YOUR HE[illegible]
[illegible]
GO ON

RECOVERING FROM HEART FAILURE

A personal story of humour, healing, and hope

Mark Stibbe

BELLA BOOKS

First published 2025 by Bella Books UK, a Pawprint/Imprint of BookLab

www.thebooklab.co.uk

British Library Cataloguing in Publication Data. A catalogue record for this book is available from the British Library.

ISBN: 978-1-0369-1501-8

Cover design by Esther Kotecha

Printed in the UK

A WORD TO THOSE WITH HEART (CARDIAC) FAILURE

If you're concerned about whether you may have this condition and you're looking for reliable information, or you have been diagnosed already and you're in need of support, the go-to UK resource is the British Heart Foundation (BHF). The BHF website offers a lot of helpful tips. You can access materials for free at https://www.bhf.org.uk. There you'll find easily digestible and insightful information on the causes, symptoms, stages, and treatment of heart failure, both in English and other languages.

The BHF is an inspiring organisation; it funds groundbreaking scientific research into heart disease; their booklet *Your Guide to Heart Failure* is essential reading; and the BHF Facebook page is a lifeline for those feeling like they're facing this alone and who want to talk to others on a similar path.

Speaking from my own experience as a patient, and my wife's experience as someone supporting a loved one with heart failure, the BHF is the best place to start.

DEDICATION

This book is dedicated to the three doctors who, in the course of one week, rescued my heart – Dr Edward Petzer, Dr Anne-Louise Vaney, and Dr Kevin Ward; to the heroic staff who looked after me at the William Harvey Hospital in Ashford; to my current heart doctor (Dr Fisher); my community heart nurse (Ann Oram); to those who work at New Lyminge Surgery (especially Tina); and to my friend, Dr Annette Slade, with unending thanks.

CONTENTS

PROLOGUE

SEVEN LIFE-CHANGING DAYS

I'm a full-time writer, but never in a thousand dreamy moments did I ever think I would one day write a book about being treated for acute heart failure. But then again, it never occurred to me that there was something wrong with my heart, even though there were, looking back, many warning signs. Pretty big ones, if I'm honest. Ones I should have heeded a lot earlier than I did.

Let me share a couple.

It's December 2023. My wife, Cherith, and I are sitting outside Hamley's toyshop in London. My oldest son and his wife, along with their two tiny children, are on a rare visit to the UK. We have all just strolled around the Natural History Museum in London, roaring back at the animatronics T-Rex with its Santa hat. Now we're about to enter my favourite toyshop in the world.

Except that I need to sit down on a wall. All I want to do is go to sleep. Even though my grandchildren mean the world to me, and I want to make the most of every fleeting second, I am depleted, desperate to be somewhere quiet and warm. I'm beyond exhausted. That was a warning sign. It's called fatigue.

A few weeks later, just after Christmas, I'm walking near home in the East Kent Downs with Cherith and our two Labradors, Bella and Phoebe. We head up a very familiar hill – not a large one – and I'm breathless. I stop six or seven times along a slope that I have negotiated many times without any difficulty. The effort feels gargantuan. I don't remember being this tired even when I climbed Scafell Pike or marched across the Brecon Beacons as an army cadet. That's another warning sign. It's called breathlessness.

I don't realise it at the time, but I am suffering some of the classic symptoms associated with heart failure. I don't even know what heart failure is, nor how common it is in the UK. Four months later, I will hear the words 'heart failure' from a local GP as she diagnoses what is wrong with me, and on the lips of the hospital staff who treat me when I am rushed to Accident and Emergency after running out of steam altogether. Only then will I begin to learn about this all-too common condition, and the measures needed to treat it.

I am happy to say that Cherith and I – along with our two Labradors – did our customary walk this morning at 6.00 a.m., and I am even happier to report that I marched up the same hill without pausing for a breather. That's how much my health has changed for the better. I have some of my old energy back. And I'm not the only one who thinks that. Two very dear friends of ours – Lauren and Kirsty, and their son Finley – visited us a few months ago. "I don't mean to be rude," Lauren said, "But you look ten years younger."

I feel it!

And I'm grateful for it.

So grateful.

Not least because my stunning wife is a lot younger than me, so my heart needs to be doing its job!

Like I said, I never anticipated I'd one day write a book like this, but then I never considered I might be one of the many, many people who suffer from heart failure. I've done some research to find out just how many. Thanks to the excellent work of the British Heart Foundation, we know the statistics, and they are getting worse. According to the latest figures, the number of people in the UK with heart failure is about 800,000. There are 200,000 new cases every year and that number is likely to rise. The ageing population and better survival rates after heart attacks are responsible in the main for this increase. Just to cheer you up even more, 1 in 35 people between 65-74 will suffer from heart failure. 1 in 15 between 75-84. 1 in 7 over 85.

I was 63 when I was rushed into hospital. There, an amazing team of heroic medics worked their socks off to diagnose exactly why my heart was failing and then insert a pacemaker and defibrillator in my chest to remedy the primary fault – a lack of synchronization between the two lower chambers, resulting in a heart rhythm and rate that was, well, crazy and, ultimately, dangerous. This state-of-the-art device, along with a course of medication that I will have to take for the rest of my life, has very likely not only saved my life but given me the chance to enjoy a healthy future. I couldn't be more grateful.

The seven days I spent receiving cardiac care were therefore life-changing. As I started to share stories about this momentous week, I was frequently told, "You should turn this into a book." "I'm sure someone's already done that," I would reply.

Then, one day, I decided to check. I conducted a search for medical memoirs (i.e., real-life stories) by people like me who had been diagnosed with heart failure and recovered. Do you know how many I found? Zero! When I searched Amazon for books about heart failure, I found volumes of a clinical nature (written for medics) and ones of a factual nature (written for patients) but no memoirs. Since stories touch our hearts far more quickly and deeply than statistics ever can, let alone studies, I was surprised. There are so many who suffer from heart failure, so many who are going to suffer from it in the future. Why are there no book-length testimonies written by patients?

One reason may well lie in the demise of the memoir itself. Publishers have become notoriously sceptical of them, unless of course they're written by a celebrity like Prince Harry or Charles Spencer. People have had their fill of what's called the "misery memoir." It's fair to say that many people need to write them more than readers need to read them. Even though these tales may be cathartic for the author, they're often neither joyful nor uplifting. That's why I decided to tell my own story with humour, hope, and a focus on healing. If you're suffering from heart failure, I want you to have a good laugh. I'd love it if my book displaced anxiety with positivity.

In the end, I decided to write this book (a) because there's a huge gap when it comes to heart-failure stories, and (b) because there's a pressing need to address what is becoming a bigger and bigger medical challenge – one that may end up affecting more lives than cancer does. I have been told that heart failure already causes more deaths than the most common cancers combined. It is also the number one reason why people over 65 are hospitalised. If we have no problem finding memoirs written by cancer patients, why is it so hard to find ones written by people with heart failure?

And then there's another reason I took up my pen. I have come to appreciate the human heart more than ever. Consider the way it generates the energy we need every day. I love a good truck. I have a dream of owning a pickup one day. One of those Ford Raptors would do me nicely. I have been reliably informed that my heart generates enough energy in one day to power a Ford Raptor for twenty miles. Over the course of my entire life, it will produce enough power to send that lovely Red Raptor I dream about to the moon and back. As Doctor Roberto Bolli, a chief cardiologist, not long ago said, "The heart is really a miraculous organ. It beats 72 times a minute throughout our life, which means billions of times in our lifetime... It is an engineering feat that never ceases to amaze me." I have always been squeamish about the human heart. Not anymore. I celebrate it!

And I celebrate those who look after our hearts when we need cardiac care. I am telling my story in a UK context. In my country, every citizen has free access to the National Health Service (NHS) and to lifesaving medical treatment. I know the NHS gets some bad press these days. The lack of investment by successive national governments, as well as poor management by some NHS trusts, has created long delays when it comes to hospital, GP, and mental-health services. This has fuelled deep resentment among many members of the public, especially because unnecessary deaths have occurred as a direct result. The social contract between the NHS and the people of Great Britain has therefore reached breaking point. Lord Ara Darzi's recent 142-page study of the NHS, commissioned by the new Labour Government, has warned that the repair and reform of the NHS will take way longer than the five years Labour promised before the general election in 2024. It's not just people like me who have been at death's door. The NHS is critically ill and in desperate need of lifesaving care.

Although righteous anger is often directed against both local and national governments for the state of the NHS, we should take great care that the heroic people on the ground – those who toil away on the wards of our hospitals – do not become collateral damage. My experiences tell me that NHS workers are often the very best of people. They are angry too. Some of the medics I describe in this book have expressed their frustrations to me. One talked about the devastating effects caused by the transition over time from a job that focused on people to one focused on paper. This top-down bureaucratization of medical care has taken the joy and meaning out of the job for them. If they resign, that will be a tragedy. Another talked to me of three weeks and weekends without a break, and the injustices caused by poor resourcing. They were heartbroken by the lack of beds for Kent patients, and the lack of space for those needing to be referred from London.

When I sent copies of a draft manuscript of this book to NHS staff, my wife and I were very moved by their replies. I had written asking them to check they were happy with the accuracy of my account, especially those parts where I mention them. They confessed to how gladdened they were not just at my recovery but also at hearing someone speaking positively about their work. I cannot begin to imagine the despondency they must feel when they're exhausted by the intensity and amount of their hours, and when they're deflated by the knowledge of how much better things could be if only there were adequate resources and better management of them. In case you are unaware of the figures, more than 7.6 million people were awaiting NHS treatment in England in December 2024. The number of people who have been forced to wait more than a year for treatment – when they should receive it within 18 weeks – has risen fifteenfold since 2010. Staying motivated in a culture like this must be very challenging.

The current Health Secretary, Wes Streeting, has called on the nation to help him shape a ten-year health plan for NHS reform. He has asked us to share ideas about what the NHS might look like, and he's requested stories from people who have good experiences of the NHS. Streeting says that the NHS saved his life when he was treated for kidney cancer in 2021. He says that we all owe the NHS a debt of gratitude. I couldn't agree more. That's why I have posted a copy of this book to him in the hope that my story will help his government provide better and proper resources for an institution which is one of the things about the UK that other countries admire and envy the most. The NHS badly needs support, both from us, its beneficiaries, and from the government. The Royal College of Nurses has reported that young people currently starting their nursing careers in hospital – Gen Z workers between 21-30 – are deeply unhappy in their roles. Between 2013-2023, their stress levels soared, as did their dissatisfaction with their pay. Many of them talk about a lack of staffing and a lack of support. The number of those leaving nursing has surged, while those applying for nursing is in freefall. I really hope this book will encourage us all to take better care of those who take such good care of us.

One final thing: I'm not a medic myself and I'm therefore not an expert in cardiac care, so don't take my treatment as the blueprint for yours. I'm not suggesting you and I are identical. Our heart conditions will be unique, and our recovery will be too. One person's testimony should therefore not become the template for another person's treatment. This is simply *my* story. It is intended to encourage you that you are not alone. People like me are on a similar trajectory to people like you. The road ahead may have some unique challenges, but with the right help you too will get a second chance to browse in a toyshop with your grandkids, or to storm a hill with your dogs.

My hope is that you will feel what I feel - that you have been given an amazing chance to begin life again. That's why I have designed this book as seven life-changing days. It's why I have quoted from the seven days of creation in Genesis 1 at the start of each section. Although at the time they were challenging, the seven days of my cardiac care were filled with creative purpose and energy. As I went through the hours that made up this week, it felt like what Proust once said, "the creation of the world... occurs every day," and I learned, as Meister Eckhart once remarked, "to trust the magic of beginnings."

If you have been diagnosed with heart failure, I send you happy thoughts and empathetic prayers. May you receive many cardiac blessings on your therapeutic journey. May you hear and believe the title of this book. With a partial debt to the wonderful Celine Dion, may you learn that "Your heart will go on."

CHAPTER 1

YOU HAVE HEART FAILURE

Those words were spoken by a GP at my local surgery. I was sitting in her office, next to my wife Cherith. Cherith had been allowed off work to hear the results of my recent blood tests and ECG.

"It's an awful phrase, 'heart failure'," the doctor added with half a smile. "It sounds so frightening. But it can be treated with medication. Please, try not to worry."

She went on to explain that the heart is like an electric pump. When it isn't working properly, that is called 'heart failure.' There can be different reasons for this - a heart attack, for example. In my case, an ECG had picked up abnormalities and irregularities in my cardiac rhythm and rate. My heart was failing for reasons unknown, and there were signs of that in my poor health.

I'll just describe one symptom I was experiencing at the time - a very unpleasant and persistent cough. I had suffered with it since before Christmas. This appointment with the doctor happened the following May, so we're talking six months. This was unlike any other cough I had ever experienced. It seemed to come from my chest, but not from my lungs. Once it started, it could become so overwhelming that it sometimes brought me to the brink of vomiting. In the middle of the night, I would awaken not only Cherith but our two Labradors, Bella and Phoebe. My hacking would often become so loud and long that I feared I would be arrested for breaching the peace in the remote, rural neighbourhood where we live in Kent.

Three weeks before the May appointment, I had gone to the same surgery and a nurse had examined my chest. She had heard what she called "a crackling sound" and put me on a course of antibiotics. Seven days of these had not shifted the cough. By the time I had finished the course, I was worse than ever. This confused me. Every time I had taken antibiotics in the past they had done the trick. This time the cough was proving stubborn, unshakable, and tenacious. Worse still, I kept remembering an NHS advert that I'd seen on social media after the Covid-19 pandemic. It said something about going to the doctor if you have a cough that lasts longer than three weeks. It could be nothing, but then, on the other hand, it could be something serious – like cancer. I remembered this because the ad was followed by a lot of sarcastic comments from people who had tried contacting their local surgery during Covid and failed to get any answer. Sitting in the doctor's room, I now found myself grateful for two things: firstly, that I had managed to navigate my way through the surgery's eConsult system online and get an appointment with a GP, which felt miraculous; secondly, that what I had was not ... well... terminal.

This was a very real and relevant issue for me. The previous autumn, I had been approached by a very dear friend of mine for help. Steve was the senior editor of *Sorted*, voted the UK's most wholesome men's magazine. I had the privilege of reviewing new Lego products for it. Steve and I had known each other for a long time. He helped me through a difficult phase when I was living alone, broke and depressed, on the West Sussex coast. United by our mutual love of dogs, we would walk our beloved canine companions along some of the best beaches in Britain, often stopping for a hearty and not altogether healthy cooked breakfast at a seaside café halfway. Steve's companionship helped me through a very tough season of my life.

Steve knew that I coached writers for a living, so he contacted me and asked if I could advise him with his new book. He had been told in April 2023 that he only had five months left to live. It was now past his designated death day in September, and he wanted to write an upbeat memoir of his medical journey over the previous two years. Being a gifted stand-up comedian, he wanted it to be positive and funny. Would I be able to guide him through the process?

It just so happened that I had taken on a ghost-writing project that was going to cover the bills for the next twelve months or so. Cherith and I were therefore in the position of knowing that we were going to be able to pay the rent and cover our overheads.

"I'd be delighted," I replied. Remembering all Steve had done for me as a mate, I said I wouldn't charge him.

Over the next few months, I became intimately acquainted with Steve's cancer. To say his journey was harrowing is an understatement, so when my own doctor told me my cough was not cancer, part of me was grateful. It pains me to add that just five months after this meeting with my GP, my mate Steve died.

"So, what's next?" Cherith asked the doctor.

"We need Mark to have an echocardiogram to assess what's really been going on with his heart."

The doctor explained that an echocardiogram is an ultrasound scan designed to study the heart and its blood vessels using echoes or high-frequency sound waves. It would be different from the ECG I had been given two days before. Although an ECG also monitors your heart, it is designed to pick up abnormalities in the electrical impulses of your heart, while an echocardiogram uses 'echoes' to detect problems with the actual structure of your heart. I needed an echocardiogram to see why my heart was functioning in such an odd way and with such obviously reduced power – hence 'heart failure.'

"When can he have one?" Cherith asked.

"I'll put in a request. If you haven't heard anything in two weeks, please get back to me."

I wrongly took comfort from this comment. I figured that if the echocardiogram could wait, then there was no urgency. Cherith was not so nonchalant. Once she heard the words "heart failure," she wanted the wheels to start moving there and then. The diagnosis sounded like my heart had given up, surrendered, ceased functioning, stopped fighting. None of these ideas provided any cause for complacency. If the diagnosis was as serious as the terminology implied, then two weeks to wait seemed to her far too long, and the possibility of people not contacting us to arrange the echocardiogram was appalling.

It's important at this point for me to stress that Cherith is not a negative or pessimistic person at all. She's not the worrying type; that's one of the reasons I fell in love with her. Having said that, for weeks she had been seeing my health decline and witnessing me deteriorate. This was especially acute at nighttime.

I want you to imagine not being able to get comfortable when you lie down in bed. You feel your chest constricting, causing you to become breathless. You try lying on one side. Same symptoms. You try the other. Same again. You try lying on your front. Just as bad. Every position is a nightmare. This goes on for weeks and weeks. Instead of bedtime being something you look forward to, as you have since you were a boy, it is now a time you dread.

You place a beanbag in one corner of your small bedroom. You steal one of the thin mattresses used by one of your two Labradors, and you slide it underneath the front end of the bean bag so that your bum won't become numb during the night. You slip into the beanbag after saying goodnight and you try to find a position that is upright enough to ease the pressure on your chest. You arrange your cough sweets and tissues on the wooden box on your left. You then slide into the gap between the box and your wife's dressing table on your right. Your two Labradors, who have not been used to having their sleeping arrangements or routines disrupted, emit several loud groans as darkness fills the room.

You sleep for a maximum of two hours before you wake up coughing again and needing to go to the toilet. You tiptoe out of the bedroom to the bathroom. You try and force some urine out of your system, but you end up knowing it's been minimal. There is still that nagging feeling of wanting to go, and then there's that cough. You stay in the toilet, hoping that you can do the simple things you've always taken for granted, like peeing and breathing.

But you can't.

Cherith has seen all this firsthand.

She is desperately worried.

She wants the echocardiogram now.

Truth be told, even I am a little concerned. The doctor has just told us that the echocardiogram will reveal what's wrong with my heart and determine what they need to do. That way, she said, "We'll know how to manage your condition in the future."

I think about these words on the drive home. I make a living from words, so words are important.

I remember the doctor said 'manage'.

Not 'cure'.

Even then, I put a spin on the word 'failure.' Over the last ten years, I have specialised in harnessing the negative power of failure and turning it into something positive. I have learned to engage in what Matthew Syed calls 'black box thinking' and turn the fault lines in my soul into life lessons designed to prevent future crashes, both for me and others. It has been a hard and harrowing decade in many ways, but it has also been the period of my life when I have learned who I really am and begun to tolerate and even celebrate the new, true version of myself. All this has been soul work. Leaving the doctor's office, I figure I now need to do some body work. It's time to mend my heart.

I am being very naïve, of course. I have received my diagnosis, yes, but what I don't realise is that there are no magic wands I can use to turn failure into success.

Cherith already senses this.
I need to as well.
I am going to need a wakeup call.

CHAPTER 2

PAUSING CLARKSON'S FARM

I've always taken the view that there's no point worrying until you know there's a reason to worry. I have lived by a principle often attributed to Sherlock Holmes – "Give me facts!" The thing is, I had already been given facts two days before my appointment with the doctor. I just didn't know what they meant or the implications.

Let me explain what happened. Two days before my trip to my local GP on May 10th, I had gone with my wife Cherith to the same surgery for three blood tests and an ECG. A nurse administered both. She told me someone would call later that day with the results. This was Wednesday May 8th, 2024.

We waited by the phone all day. In the end, the nurse called me early evening just before the surgery closed. She was very apologetic. "The doctor's too busy to call," she said. "She's asked me to read the notes she's scribbled on your ECG print out."

Once again, I felt optimistic. If the nurse was conveying the news rather than the doctor, maybe my problems weren't as bad as I thought. Once again, I was entirely wrong.

"It's not easy to read," she continued. "But I think it says... *Left axis deviation. RBBB. Bifascicular block. Irregular pulse.*"

"What does all that mean?" I asked.

"I have no idea," she replied.

I was so tired and confused after this call that I didn't know where to start. Fortunately, my wife Cherith is like a dog with a bone in these situations, so she started doing what some people regard as questionable – yes, you guessed it, she began searching for answers on what my Northern Irish mother-in-law once referred to as '*the* Google.' This just added to the confusion. If the notes had identified just one issue or symptom, Cherith might have had a chance of getting somewhere. But the list of problems the doctor had identified made this all but impossible. We were left to guess, and our guessing wasn't hopeful. Nouns like 'block' and 'deviation' did not fill us with enthusiasm. Nor did the adjective 'irregular.'

"The doctor wants to see you," the nurse concluded.

"When?"

"In two days. Friday May 10th. 11.00am."

"I'll be there," I said.

When the nurse ended the call, Cherith and I reacted in different ways. She spent the next 36 hours worrying she was going to lose me. I took the attitude that there was no point worrying until Friday. When Friday came, the doctor explained what her notes had meant, but I still couldn't understand what was blocked, what was deviating, and why my pulse was so irregular. All Cherith and I could hear was 'heart failure.' Everything else went over our heads.

On Sunday evening, Cherith and I sat down next to each other on the sofa and started watching the season finale of *Clarkson's Farm* – one of our favourite shows. Some way into the episode, I became aware that Cherith was not looking at the TV.

She was looking at me.

Expecting her to be smiling, which I had often found her doing in the past, I saw tears pouring down her face. I ought to say here that Cherith is a red-headed Northern Irish woman possessing a formidable backbone of steel, extraordinary resilience, and a Celtic warrior spirit. At our wedding reception in 2015, I had praised her for being the grittiest person I had met.

"Are you okay?" I asked, pausing the programme.

She shook her head.

"What's up?"

"I'm worried about you." She managed to get the words out between tears.

"Why now?"

"I've been worried about you for days."

It turns out that Cherith had phoned her mother after the appointment with the doctor. She had tried to communicate what the doctor said about heart failure. "It's looking bad, Mum," she said. "I don't think Mark realizes."

Late that same Sunday afternoon, Cherith came out of the house into our back garden. It was a sunny day, and I was sitting on a chair on the patio just behind our little house. Later she was to tell me that I had a look she had never seen on my face before. I was staring into the middle distance with my mouth half open. "It was as if you had just enough energy to keep your chin from falling. You were just surviving. Existing. Hanging on. I was so worried about you."

Now, here we were watching *Clarkson's Farm* and hearing about Gerald's fight with a life-threatening illness. The whole nation, it seemed, was rooting for him. All this talk of sickness, coupled with my fatigue, had brought Cherith to the brink.

"You've got to take this seriously," Cherith said, the tears streaming down her face.

"Let's see what tomorrow brings," I replied. "Maybe the doctor will fix me up for that echocardiogram sooner rather than later. Then we'll really know what we're dealing with."

I promised her I would take things seriously. I swore I would respect her feelings. But deep down, I still harboured a hope that this was a storm in a teacup, and that medication would make the whole thing go away. Maybe nature would take its course and my body's own systems would repair what needed to be repaired. Maybe I would have a good night's sleep and wake up feeling a lot better the next morning. I switched off the TV, leaving Clarkson paused, and went to bed, hoping my wishes would come true.

I couldn't have been more wrong.

DAY 1
MONDAY

MAY 13TH 2024

And there was evening, and there was morning - the first day.

Genesis 1:5

CHAPTER 3

IN-LAWS FROM HEAVEN

I got up the next morning, Monday May 13th, feeling rough - really rough. I had struggled all night to ease the pressure on and in my chest. I tried breathing through my nose, then my mouth. Neither eased the discomfort. I tried positioning myself at every imaginable angle in the beanbag in the corner of the bedroom. Still no relief. I ditched the beanbag and returned to my side of the bed, hoping not to wake Cherith, desperate to win the battle to breathe. Still no better. In the end, I fell asleep more from exhaustion than anything else. This was two hours before the alarm went – the Monday-to-Friday signal for Cherith to get up and head to work at a school in Canterbury. When I opened my eyes, I started coughing once again, as I had numerous times in the night. Sitting upright on the edge of my side of the bed did not bring any respite. I felt so damn tired.

Cherith turned to me and said, "I've got a really bad headache."

I knew straightaway this was stress.

"I can't go to work like this," she added.

I nodded, relieved she was going to stay at home.

"I'm not leaving you in this state either."

Cherith called work and her boss Julia – ever understanding and supportive – wished her a speedy recovery from what was building towards a migraine. In the end, Cherith didn't have time to allow her headache to develop into something worse. My condition was about to deteriorate rapidly.

I don't know if you remember the original *Star Trek* series with William Shatner as Captain Kirk and Leonard Nimoy as Spock. I grew up riveted to this series in the sixties and seventies. In most episodes, the story would involve a scene or two in sickbay where the moody doctor – Leonard McCoy, acted by DeForrest Kelley – looked after his patients on beds that had screens above them. In the original series, these screens were body-function scanners that recorded the pulse, respiration, temperature, bloods, and brain activity of the patient. When someone was dying, the arrows recording these vital signs would descend until the point of expiration. The task given to 'Bones' (McCoy's nickname) was to make sure he administered treatment before the arrows in these six columns reached the bottom. Fun fact: the monitors now used in real-life hospitals are inspired by these scanners.

During Monday morning, it was as if I was in the sickbay of the Enterprise and all six arrows were descending. Towards lunchtime, I lay down on the bed. Something was going on in my head. It felt like my brain activity was shutting down and that if I stayed inactive any longer, I wouldn't be able to stop the descent and deterioration. I had to do something. It felt like I was dying.

My sense of urgency was intensified when I received an NHS text. This informed me that if I hadn't received a message arranging my appointment for the echocardiogram by June 10th, I was to contact them and let them know. That concerned me. June 10th was weeks away and the thought that I might have to join the end of another queue and wait another month for tests was too much for me to handle. I managed to stand up and head to the door. My head stopped spinning and the strange sense of what I can only describe as a kind of 'brain tinnitus' decreased. I called out to Cherith for help.

Cherith rushed to me, worry etched on her tired face. I told her I was now desperate to get proper medical care. This was what she was waiting to hear. Now she could act.

Unknown to me, after the doctor had told me I had heart failure, Cherith had received a message from her mum.

"I've had a word with your father," her mum had said. "If Mark needs a private appointment, we'll pay for that."

I was as relieved as I was grateful to hear this. I asked Cherith to see what could be arranged.

Cherith rang KIMS – a private hospital just outside Maidstone, about 45 minutes away from where we live in Kent. She got through to a woman in cardiology.

"We've got availability on Thursday," she said.

Maybe she detected the worry in Cherith's voice; she hesitated before we had a chance to say yes.

"Could you hold for a moment. The cardiologist is in today. I'll just have a word with him."

She was back within a minute.

"Could you make 5.30pm this afternoon?"

I nodded and Cherith secured the slot.

A few hours later, we arrived at KIMS and headed to the office of one of the finest cardiologists in the UK. Dr Edward Petzer asked me what my symptoms were. He did not react with any alarm when I told him. I thought maybe things weren't as bad after all. Then I remembered that the man holding the stethoscope was an experienced consultant who had listened to my kind of testimony multiple times. He was trained not to react. I was not wise in the head trying to get any kind of tell from his eyes or his face, let alone from his voice.

After he had completed his initial examination, he looked at me with professional concern.

"Your heartrate is all over the place," he said, his voice calm. "Are you aware of this?"

I nodded that I was.

"Do you mind if I do an ECG?" he asked.

"Go right ahead."

He left the room leaving us both wondering what all this meant. Moments later, he returned. He was not alone. Behind him was a nurse pushing a portable ECG monitor.

"Please take off your shirt," he said.

Seconds later I was on a bed in his office, and a nurse was attaching wires to various sites in and around my chest. He gave the signal to the nurse to start the readings. When the scan was complete, I heard a sheet of paper being printed and emerging from the machine. The doctor took it in his hands and studied it.

When he spoke, he repeated some of the phrases we had heard the nurse read out from my doctor's notes the previous week. This was followed by his recommended course of action.

"You need to go to A&E."

It was at this point I asked a stupid question.

"When?"

Somehow, my brain had forgotten that the word emergency in A&E denoted this would be happening now.

"Can you drive him there?" he asked Cherith.

"I need to fill up with petrol," she said.

The doctor gave her directions to the nearest petrol station.

Cherith hurried from the room.

"An ambulance will take at least three hours," he said. "If your wife takes you, you'll be there in under half an hour. You need to get to the William Harvey Hospital, and you need to get there fast. We don't provide acute care here. You'll be safe there."

That little word 'safe' made a big impact on me. I knew from that moment that I wasn't safe at home. I needed to be admitted to the William Harvey Hospital in Ashford. I would be surrounded by people and instruments that could save my life.

With the doctor escorting me, I managed to walk down several corridors towards the exit. I had to stop several times to get my breath back, but eventually I made it.

I paused to go the men's toilet, figuring it might be a while before I had the chance to go again. When I came out, the doctor and Cherith were waiting. According to Cherith, I had an air of nonchalance, as if I was coming out of a toilet at a cinema or a restaurant. That was because I had just looked at my reflection in the mirror above the basin where I washed my hands. I looked terrible, yes. My eyes looked exhausted and my skin pale. But the doctor had used the word 'safe.' I was in good hands, and I was about to be in the best hands. It felt like great people were looking out for me – that I was being held and upheld by a peace and a power far greater than me.

And Cherith felt the same.

When Cherith arrived at the petrol station just minutes before this, she had been overwhelmed by a sense of relief. She was worried sick while I was at home, not taking matters as seriously as she was. Now we were heading to hospital, the weight of that worry lifted. I was facing reality, and I was heading somewhere where I would be, well, *safe*. Thanks to the generosity and kindness of her parents, I was going to be given that echocardiogram I needed.

By this time, I had been married to Cherith for almost nine years and had known my parents-in-law for that time and longer. I had never told them what they meant to me, so it was time to say something. This is what I wrote to my Irish in-laws:

'I'm not very good at this, being from the Stoical stiff upper lip ranks of the English (an inferior race, I know), but I want to say how much I really appreciate your love and care. It has been very humbling and at times a little disorientating seeing how much I mean to people like your good selves, and to the rest of my now very beloved and much appreciated Irish family.

I'd like you to know that I love you both too. I may not say it, and I may find it hard to demonstrate, but that doesn't mean I don't feel it. I do. And I regard your inclusion and acceptance of me as one of the greatest and most undeserved gifts of my life.

Thank you for your love. Know that this Englishman

is honoured to be on the receiving end of it. And it is reciprocated in my own understated way xx.'

CHAPTER 4

DRIVE LIKE AN AMBULANCE

While I had been in the toilet, Doctor Edward was giving Cherith some instructions. The first was to give me a small aspirin, which she did. The second was to take me straight to A&E.

"Drive like an ambulance," he said. Making sure she understood, he added, "No jolts or bumps."

I'm pretty sure Cherith mainly heard the first part - about driving like an ambulance - because as soon as we left the carpark, she was pressing down on the accelerator and rushing to the M20. As we hit the motorway, all I could think of was the way she played PlayStation games such as *Grand Turismo 7* and *Grand Theft Auto 5*. Several times she had stolen an ambulance while playing the role of Trevor in GTA. I had visions of her repeating his behaviour and knocking down lampposts and pedestrians while racing to the hospital.

"Please slow down," I said. "If we're stopped for speeding,

it'll tip me over the edge."

Cherith, who was in her own zone at this point, somehow heard me and settled at a more sensible speed.

After less than thirty minutes, we arrived at a bay reserved for ambulances outside A&E at the William Harvey Hospital. She sat me down in the foyer opposite three windows behind each of which there was a busy receptionist trying to process patients. It was Monday May 13th, about 6.30pm, and I could not believe how busy it was. There were injured and sick people hobbling in and out of the entrance on my right. The room to my left where everyone was waiting to be seen was packed with patients. I could not see a single free seat.

After reparking the car, Cherith walked up to the first window – the one on the left. "I know you're very busy, but my husband has been sent here from KIMs private hospital in Maidstone. Can someone see him as soon as possible please."

She presented the woman with the letter Doctor Edward had written about my condition and given us before we left KIMs. The receptionist scanned it then handed it back.

"He'll be seen soon," she said.

Cherith came and sat next to me, keeping one eye on the receptionist while checking I was okay. When the woman she had just spoken to then showed no sign of taking any action, Cherith headed for the middle window. She explained the situation and handed over the letter. She was met by the same response.

After waiting about fifteen minutes, Cherith walked to the third and final of the windows, on the right of the three. This time she added, "The doctor who saw him at KIMs indicated that my husband was in danger of having a heart attack."

That was true, and the lady behind this window displayed genuine concern and compassion.

"Can I see his notes?" she asked.

Cherith handed over the letter.

She read the doctor's comments.

"Leave it with me," she said.

I was watching all this play out, marvelling at my wife's dogged determination to get a reaction. It all felt to me like a surreal fairy tale. Something like this: "Once upon a time, there was a lady whose husband was very ill. She went to a castle to get help. This castle was guarded by three women. Each of them sat with stern faces in three separate booths. Only if one of them said yes could you enter.

The lady in question brought her sick husband to these female guardians. When she approached the first booth, she found the woman disinterested in her plight.

She plucked up courage and walked to the second but found this woman was too busy to help.

She was tempted to give up, but then she remembered how much she loved the sick man she had brought with her, so she headed to the third booth. There the woman proved to be kind and caring. She got up from her seat, left her station, and went to find a man with healing gifts. She spoke to him, and he nodded. The drawbridge lowered and the devoted lady led the sick man whom she loved into a courtyard. There she found all the sick people waiting to see the man with the magical gift. The lady stayed with her husband until she was sure he was going to receive the help he needed.

That's how much she loved him."

Back to the real world, Cherith's efforts paid off; not long afterwards, my name was called.

I shuffled over to the large room on my left and found a seat. After some time, a nurse came to see me. He carried a chart and was pulling behind him some kind of portable monitor designed to assess vital signs. He asked me four or five questions and wrote some notes on the chart. Then he took my blood pressure and recorded it.

"Another nurse will see you soon," he said.

The nurses he was referring to were working at stations opposite me. They were all standing or sitting at booths with the word TRIAGE written above them. They were calling people from all around me one by one and asking them questions. As I studied the others in the room, I began to wonder how long it would take before I would be seen. There were all sorts of people with all manner of problems. Some of these seemed to me to be worse than others.

During this time, several incidents stand out in my memory. The first was a young man being escorted out of the hospital by two men who looked like police officers, but who were almost certainly hospital security. The young man was in handcuffs and had been making a disturbance, abusing those who were working there, whose sole purpose was to help people like him. I remember feeling sad that hospitals had to spend money that could go towards patient care on controlling the toxic behaviour of troublemakers. I thought of my mother – a ward sister at Great Ormond Street during WW 2 – and I wondered what she would make of all this. A small part – infinitesimally small – was grateful she wasn't still alive to see such things.

The second thing I remember was a couple in their early thirties. She was in a wheelchair suffering from a head injury. They were both drunk. She had fallen and hit her head. He was sitting next to me while Cherith was playing her part in the story of the three windows. At one point, he looked at me.

"Keep an eye on her, mate. I'm just going outside. Don't let her drop off. She's got to stay awake."

I didn't have time to explain that I was not a hospital employee, nor that I was struggling to stay awake myself. The guy was determined to go outside and have a fag, and as far as he was concerned, entitled as much to receive help from me as the NHS.

I did keep an eye on the young woman.

I did manage to keep her awake.

And to be fair to the bloke, he did say thank you.

But it was all a bit of an eyeopener. No wonder the three women behind their windows were a little guarded. If they had to put up with abuse and entitlement all the time, it's no surprise they reacted to Cherith the way they did.

After an hour or so of waiting, I was summoned to see a nurse at the triage station. She took some more notes after asking me some more questions, then informed me that I would soon be called to have a blood test and an ECG.

By now Cherith and I had been in A&E for over two hours and the room was not getting any emptier. I remember thinking that all these sick people were like shark's teeth. When one was removed, another seemed to appear from nowhere to take its place.

I was beginning to feel concerned.

When would it be my turn to be seen?

CHAPTER 5

I HATE NEEDLES

In my former work life, I was a Church-of-England vicar. For over twenty years, I visited the sick and, if I'm honest, hated that part of the job. My own experiences of being a patient didn't exactly help. For example, when I was in my late 40s, and after fathering four children it was time to get the snip and become a member of what my mates called the Silver Scissors Club. On arrival, the surgeon instructed me to shave the relevant area of my anatomy. He gave me a small, blue, plastic razor - one of those disposable ones. I was nervous and it snapped.

"Just to let you know," he said. "I have some students observing the procedure. You're all right with that?"

My heart said no, but my head said yes.

Before I knew it, I was on a bed in the presence of four extra medical students, and I was revealing all. The procedure was over quickly. I was sewn up and sent home.

Two days later, I took my daughter to see a film she had

been eagerly anticipating – *Spice Girls: The Movie* (the things you do for love as a father). Halfway through, I felt so ill I thought I was dying. I had never, up to that point, experienced anything like it. I knew it wasn't the film, although I'm sure at least some of you may be thinking it was. No, there was something wrong with my groin. A thudding pain was reverberating from my right testicle. Not wanting to upset my daughter, I whispered that I was going to the loo and, once inside a Warner Brothers cubicle, took down my trousers. What greeted me was so disturbing I had to keep myself from fainting. My right testicle had swollen to the size of an avocado. I clearly had some kind of infection.

As it turned out, I had sepsis.

The next day, I travelled under blue lights to High Wycombe hospital and was subjected to tests. I have always had a phobia of blood tests. I hated them so much that anything associated with them would bring me out in a cold sweat. I never even allowed anyone to touch my elbow area because in my head that part of my body was where blood was drawn, and I didn't want anyone reminding me of that, even if the action being performed was supposed to be pleasant.

Somehow, I allowed the nurse to take my blood. I think looking back I was just too sick to rebel or refuse. When I was taken up to a bed in the intensive care ward, I had to endure the insertion of a canula and the setting up of a drip. Knowing this was necessary for me to have a chance of my testicle returning to its normal shape and size, not to mention staying alive, I looked away, closed my eyes, and surrendered. To make the experience just a little bit more challenging, the sister in charge of us all was a Pentecostal

Christian. Once I had settled, she strode into our unit and announced, "We have a vicar on the ward, so he'll pray for you lot if you want him to."

Great, I thought. *I've never wanted more to be under cover, or under the covers. I've never longed so much to be left alone. And now here I am with a new parish and a new congregation in the heart of High Wycombe hospital.*

This incident is one of the reasons I feared hospitals, especially if it meant receiving treatment. I hated cannulas, injections, and tests – especially blood tests. It was this fear of needles in general and blood tests in particular that had caused me to put off going to my GP until I – and indeed Cherith – had no choice. Only when it was painfully obvious how poorly I was, only in short when I was desperate, did I initiate the process that had led me to the A&E department of the William Harvey Hospital on this Monday night. When it came to blood tests, I wasn't ever going to allow someone to administer one as a matter of routine. I was going to have to be – what was the word Doctor Edward used? – yes, 'acute.' And acute was what I now was.

Let's go back two weeks. When I had been given three blood tests at the surgery, the nurse had found it hard to find a vein, making the process more painful. Cherith had been sitting next to me. I looked away from the nurse and asked my wife to talk to me. Cherith is one of these people who cannot converse on demand. She is allergic to small talk, which is one of the reasons I adore her. She is also someone who doesn't suffer fools gladly. Now, put on the spot, she didn't know what to say or how to say it. She stuttered and stumbled, trying to find something trivial but distracting to say, but failed so miserably that it was funny. This did the trick. My attention was diverted from the rather clumsy operation taking place on my right. I was too entertained to feel anything more than a prick, which is probably how I came across to Cherith as I laughed at her efforts.

But at least her efforts had worked.

Now, as we were sitting together on this Monday night in hospital, I was in that same headspace again. *I'm going to have more tests. That means bloods. Better prepare yourself.* Once again, I had three, each one separated by an hour, each one accompanied by Cherith's attempts at small talk, each one followed by an ECG. These blood tests were designed to assess the levels of Troponin proteins in my blood – proteins which reveal the amount of damage done to the heart muscles. When someone has a heart attack, these levels increase suddenly and dramatically. When someone has not had a shock (i.e., a heart attack), they rise gradually. Mine had been rising slowly that Monday evening. They started at 31, went to 34, then 37.

After the third blood test and ECG, I was summoned to see a very patient doctor called John. He explained what he was seeing from my bloods and ECG. "The levels are going up in your blood. They're not going up dramatically. But they are still going up."

"What are you going to do?" Cherith asked. She was determined that I wasn't going home.

"We'll do one more blood test followed by an ECG in an hour. If the levels are still climbing, then your husband will have to stay and I'm afraid he won't be going home."

I could feel Cherith willing the levels to rise.

And they did.

Just after midnight, we went to see John. He could not

have done more for us. At the previous meeting, he had asked if we had eaten anything. When we said no, he brought us some sandwiches in the waiting room. Now we were sitting with him at his desk once again. He showed us the readings. "You mustn't go home," he said, his eyes and voice as kind as they had been on the previous visit to his makeshift office. "We need to admit you."

"Good," Cherith said.

Even I breathed a sigh of relief.

The castle gates had opened, and I was in.

I told Cherith that she needed now to go home. She was very reluctant to do that and insisted that she was staying with me until I was given a bed, but we had two Labradors who needed her, so I said no. I added that I was not likely to get a bed anytime soon.

In the end, we came to a compromise. Cherith would return home, settle the dogs, and pack me a bag. She would then return, give me the bag, and then head back home to snatch a few hours sleep. I remember feeling utterly amazed by her dedication and devotion, not just to me, but to our beloved Labradors.

While Cherith was away, a nurse summoned me for yet another blood test and a further ECG. When they were over, I realised that I hadn't been anxious of either. I wasn't afraid of needles. I wasn't afraid of having my blood pressure measured. I wasn't afraid of hospitals. I wasn't afraid of what lay ahead, whatever that looked like. All the fears that had made me reluctant to seek help in the past seemed to have disappeared.

The emotional blockages in my heart had gone. Now it was time for the physical ones to be dealt with too.

CHAPTER 6

THE LONGEST DAY

Cherith and I eventually parted at 3.00a.m. in a ward called 'Triage and Major Assessments.' I had seen the word 'triage' already in A&E. I could not recall seeing or hearing that word since the opening scenes of *Saving Private Ryan*. There, at the D-Day landings, Captain Miller (Tom Hanks) was attempting to capture the first lines of German defence while enemy machine gunners caused carnage among the men around him. The US medics were assessing the wounded while staying undercover. In the chaos, they were conducting their own triage, working out who was dead, who was unlikely to survive, who could be saved. It is a harrowing scene, one that sticks in the memory especially if you saw it, as I did, on the big screen. Thanks to the hand-held camera work, you feel as if you are there, cowering behind the small walls of sand.

I had arrived at the William Harvey Hospital at 6.30pm on Monday evening. It was now the early hours of Tuesday morning, and I was sitting in a bed-less ward designed as a triage station. I'll never forget my walk there. Following the well-lit signs, I started the trek down several very long corridors. I think it may well have been a combination of the tiredness I was feeling from the day's events, and the fatigue that I had been living with because of my heart failure, but this short walk turned out to be an Olympic challenge. I became so breathless after only a few steps that I had to find somewhere to sit and recover. I repeated this manoeuvre about six or seven times on my way to the Triage ward, pausing in alcoves and side rooms, finding anything resembling a chair where I could summon one more drop of fuel from a tank that was already registering 'Empty'. Somehow, I made it to my destination. It had been an epic journey.

As I navigated the restless hours before dawn, I tried to get some sleep. I was, after all, sitting upright, as I had at home in the beanbag. This eased the tightness in my chest, so that was a plus. There was, however, a very big minus - a loud and disruptive patient. That was not something I was used to at home.

I had spotted the man in A&E. He had been trying to impress a girl sitting opposite him and two girls sitting directly behind him. From what I could make out, he was pretending to talk to someone on his phone. From the reaction of the two girls, who were trying not to laugh out loud, he was not talking to anyone at all but engaged in some Walter Mitty fantasy in which he was pretending to talk to a music producer and acting the part of a bass player in a heavy metal band. While he was engaged in this fantastical conversation, he used his free hand to engage in a slap-bass mime. In his own eyes, he looked cool, but in everyone else's, he looked like a muppet.

When I was transferred by the soft-spoken Dr John from A&E to the Triage and Majors ward, I had entertained the rather foolish thought that the show-off would not be coming to the same assessment area. How wrong I was. No sooner had Cherith and I kissed each other goodbye, than the slap-bass muppet arrived in the ward. This had been nice and quiet up to that point, and some of the thirty or so patients in the room had been falling asleep. I harboured the hope of being one of these blessed nappers, but any chance of that was ruined by the muppet's entrance. He had enjoyed the clearly unfamiliar experience of a captive audience in A&E, and he equally clearly had no intention of ignoring the potential for the same in the Triage and Majors ward. So, off he went around the ward, addressing his adoring fans one by one, circulating and talking – no shouting – as he invaded the new space. I leaned my head against the wall and sighed. There was only thing for it. I was going to have to pretend to sleep.

Fortunately, this seemed to work. The muppet passed me by and worked his noisy way around the room until he found a seat free next to the two girls who had been sitting behind him in A&E, grinning as he had mimicked John Paul Jones of *Led Zeppelin*. These poor creatures were now subjected to a semi-drunken monologue designed for everyone else to hear. I don't think there was a single soul in that ward who wasn't wishing – and in my case praying – for the muppet to fall asleep, but our wishes and prayers were not quickly granted. On and on he talked, until eventually, at about 5.30am, the girls decided they both needed the toilet at the same time. Only then did the muppet drape his body over one of their now-vacant chairs and promptly fall asleep. There was something almost endearing in this; he reminded me of one of my boys when he was a toddler; he could pivot from extreme activity to deep sleep in the matter of a nanosecond.

But there the likeness stopped. Within seconds, the muppet show changed from one form of noise to another. I don't think I have ever, in my 63 years, heard anyone snore as loudly as this man. It was as if some large, draconian beast had taken up residence in the bowels of the hospital. It was an indoor sonic boom.

"He's louder asleep than he is awake," muttered one elderly lady, whose weariness seemed more emotional than physical. We all smiled. We had already spotted the irony.

As a parenthesis, I am aware that my comments here may appear very rude and disrespectful.

So, let me just say, before moving on, that I am a great fan of the Muppets, especially Floyd Pepper, the bass player, and that I mean no offence either to them or to him.

No sooner had this human muppet fallen asleep than I was summoned for more treatment. It was now approaching 6.00a.m. and a nurse fitted a cannula to my left arm. She administered three injections via the cannula, at least one of which was designed to flush the excess fluid out of my system.

She then produced a fourth syringe.

"What's that one for?" I asked.

"Blood thinner," she said.

I assumed this was also going to go through the cannula and be as painless as the previous three.

"This one's in the tummy," she muttered.

I remember shuddering when she said this. I had never, up until this moment, had an injection in my stomach, but I had heard of people who had, and their testimonies always made me squeamish. This was a real test for me. Was I really freed from my fear of needles? Would I be able to go through with this?

I think it helped at this point that the nurse was not in the mood for dillydallying. She was exhausted and just wanted her patients to comply. I was exhausted too, so I think our combined fatigue just fortified our zoned-out detachment.

I rolled up the bottom of my T-shirt and let her inject me. I even watched the needle go into my diminishing waistline, watching its entrance and exit as if it was all happening to someone else. I didn't feel a thing. It was over before I had time to think about it. (Fun fact; a medical friend of mine called Julian has since informed me that injections hurt less if you watch them – even true for little children!).

The nurse told me to go back to the ward where I made sure I sat as far away from the snoring muppet as I could. I found a quiet and relatively uncrowded corner and sat in a hard chair. A woman pushing a trolly offered me something to drink and eat. I gratefully accepted a cup of tea and a cheese sandwich.

I was past the point of sleep now, as was everyone else, so I turned to a couple in their early seventies (I estimated) who were still awake. It turned out the husband was the patient. He was waiting for a bed. She was his wife, determined to stay with him until he was, like the harvest grain, 'safely gathered in'. He had been a car mechanic all his working life and showed me photographs of classic cars he had restored in his spare time. I was genuinely impressed. My biological father, whom I have never met, was a car mechanic, and I have always had this deep-seated and innate respect for people who can repair and restore cars. It's one of two things I know about him. The other is that he had a career in petty crime. He was nicked for stealing hub caps, no doubt for the vehicles he restored for himself.

I looked at my phone. It was coming up to 6.30am. At last, a nurse called my name. She led me out of the ward – leaving the snoring dragon in my wake – and along a corridor. As we went, she said that my wife had just phoned her to ask how I was.

"I've told her your levels are still rising, so we're keeping a close eye on you and working to get you a bed," she said, adding, "Your wife sounds really nice."

I told her she'd caught her on a good day.

Within minutes I was upstairs on a gurney in what was called the Rapid Assessment Ward. I sent a quick text to my really nice wife to tell her I was still in the triage system.

One of the nurses adjusted my pillows so that I could be upright enough not to feel breathless.

I thought back to the start of the previous day and remembered waking up at home, fatigued; I recalled the middle of the day, thinking I was dying; then the afternoon, and Doctor Edward telling me I needed to go to A&E; finally, the evening, being triaged. It had been the longest and toughest day I could remember.

When I was a boy, I saw a black-and-white film about the Normandy landings called *The Longest Day* (1962). That too seemed to go on forever (just under 180 minutes, to be precise). Monday had gone on forever and Tuesday was already over six hours old. It was now nearly 7.00am and I hadn't slept since the few hours I had managed to snatch on Sunday night. If I thought I was going to fall asleep now, I was mistaken. Another very long day lay ahead.

DAY 2
TUESDAY

MAY 14TH 2024

And there was evening, and there was morning - the second day.

Genesis 1:8

CHAPTER 7

WELCOME TO THE MACHINES

Tuesday began with nurses rigging me up to a cardiac monitor on the left side of the gurney where I lay. This machine was designed to watch the electrical activity of my heart. It did this through a constellation of electrodes which the nurses placed on my body. Using small stickers, they stuck the electrodes to various parts of my chest and then checked the screen was registering how my heart was behaving. The same data was transmitted to a screen at the station in the main ward where it was monitored by the staff.

I was fortunate to be in a side room with a curtain. I was aware of a lot of patients in the main ward beyond. Some were lying on beds in the corridor directly outside my room. Most were in bays where they could be monitored by machines. I remember feeling very lucky to have at least a modicum of privacy.

And a *modicum* was all that I could expect. One of the injections I had been given in triage four hours before was designed to flush the excess fluid out of my system. The persistent cough that I had endured for many months was due to a buildup of fluid around my heart and in my limbs. My hands, abdomen, legs, ankles, and feet were all really swollen; they had been like this far longer than I had realised. This too was due to carrying excess fluid. The only way I could expel this was through urinating. Thanks to the injection, I was now no longer going a little and often; I was going a lot and often. This required me asking for some help. The toilet was down the corridor on my left, but I was now tied to a cardiac monitor by leads.

The only solution was for me to have something to use in my room. One of my sympathetic nurses took charge of the situation and brought a bunch of cardboard receptacles, with a funnel at one end and a cavity at the other. Sitting on the edge of my bed, I could remain in contact with the cardiac monitor while peeing into the receptacle. This I did frequently, thanks to the furosemide jab earlier, which was now working very efficiently as a diuretic. This caused such a furious flow that I feared the receptacle known as *the disposable male urinal* would not be large enough. In fact, it wasn't long before all four of these curved, artefacts needed replacing.

By now, Cherith had arrived with a tall Costa coffee from the café in the entrance area of the hospital. She had texted to ask me if I needed anything. I had replied without thinking. When she arrived, she was carrying large lattés for us both.

"Is it okay if he has this?" she asked the nurse.

"It is, but he can't drink more than 1.5 litres every 24 hours. We're trying to get rid of his excess fluid. That's why he's got so much swelling in his body right now."

The nurse showed Cherith the measuring jug of water on the portable side table next to my gurney.

"That takes one litre. He's only allowed the equivalent of another half of that once he's finished that one."

She continued speaking while she checked my electrodes. She was at the very end of her shift and doing a great job disguising how tired she was. I said *great*. I didn't say *perfect*. The next minute she looked down and checked my cannula.

"You've got fat hands," she muttered, not realizing she was talking out loud.

She apologised. "That sounded rude."

I laughed. So did Cherith. For some reason, it was just the kind of humour we needed. We knew it wasn't a comment about my weight. It was the nurse's way of noting my excess fluid. But it was so blunt that it made both of us laugh.

After that, I was determined to ensure my hands didn't get any fatter – or my feet for that matter.

I didn't touch my coffee once.

Cherith and I were now left alone. I was fascinated by the strange machine on my left with all its beeping, numbers, and signals. Every so often, the cardiac monitor would emit an alarm. To begin with, I thought this was due to worrying changes in my heartrate and rhythm, but our kind, honest-speaking nurse told us that it was more likely a poor connection or a low battery.

It turned out from this point to be a day devoted to machines. There was firstly the noisy cardiac monitor. Then, secondly, there was the blood test man. I'm sorry. I forget his name. But he was a cool looking guy – at least as I remember him – with an aging hippy vibe. He was wheeling a portable machine.

"You've seen one of these before, I take it," he said in a laid-back and friendly voice.

He produced what looked like a portable ultrasound machine.

I nodded.

"I use this to find the best vein," he said.

He proceeded to scan the elbow region of my right arm while looking at the monitor he had brought.

"There you are!" he muttered.

I looked to my left at Cherith. We were both too tired to engage in distracting small talk, so I just closed my eyes.

I felt nothing.

Mister Blood Test Man had found the perfect vein. The procedure was done before I knew it. It was the most painless and relaxing blood test I had ever had before, or since. So, whoever you are on the Rapid Assessment Ward, the guy with the portable ultrasound, you have a superpower, and I salute you.

After Blood Test Man left, I became aware that I needed a poo, so Cherith called for the nurse.

"I'll bring a commode," the nurse said.

This was one of those rare moments during my seven-day stay when I kicked up any kind of a fuss.

"I can't poo in here," I said.

You need to know that I am a bit precious about privacy when it comes to pooing. This goes right back to my early boarding school days. When I was eight, I had to join a queue of boys my age after breakfast every day for at least the first year. One by one we would have to enter a solitary toilet and attempt to poo. We would come out after the allotted time and be compelled to report to a very stern senior matron whether we had fulfilled our mission.

"Been successful?" she would ask.

Whatever we answered, she would tick or cross the relevant column in her notebook.

"Washed your hands?"

Once again, she got scribbling with a pencil after we had delivered our timid answers.

I cannot tell you what effect this has had on me for the entire duration of my life. It made me pathologically allergic to pooing in public toilets or on demand. Faced now with pooing in a side ward, I could not stomach having another matronly figure watching over my performance, nor could I cope with trying to go through the whole process while attached by some leads to a computer. I needed a modicum – there's that word again – of liberty and privacy.

"Okay, but you can't go to the toilet on your own," the nurse said. "Your wife will have to go with you."

She smiled wearily and disconnected the leads. Cherith then held me by the arm and escorted me down the corridor to the toilet door. I told her to stay outside.

"No!" she insisted. "The nurse told me to stay with you."

"As far as the door," I said.

"No. I'm going in too."

"Then I'm not doing it."

"Listen," she said. "I don't want to be in there with you any more than you want me in there with you."

I reluctantly agreed.

There then followed a few minutes in which Cherith volunteered to stand in the far corner with her face to the wall while I tried to at least get something out of my system. In the end, I managed to be marginally successful and to wash my hands.

My school matron would have been proud of me.

Back I shuffled to the gurney to be reattached to the five electrodes. When I lay down, I was exhausted by the journey to and from the toilet, and all the stress associated with it. I lay my head on the raised pillow and closed my eyes.

I was about to surrender to a welcome nap when two new staff members entered pushing another medical machine. They introduced themselves as cardiology nurses.

"This is an echocardiogram," they said.

As soon as they uttered these words, it was like an epiphany. This was the machine for which we had been waiting – *longing*, even. Cast your mind back to the previous day – Monday – and the text I had received from the NHS.

The clinic is reviewing your referral

What happens now?

You do not need to do anything at this stage.

You will be contacted by the clinic if you need to be seen and offered an appointment.

If you don't hear from them by Monday 10 June 2024, call them on 01227 206680.

Lines are open Mon to Fri - 9am to 5pm.

Your clinic details

Clinic
RAS Cardio Diagnostics - Echocardiogram (WHH Ashford)-East Kent Hospitals Trust-RVV

Your referral details

Referred by
[redacted]

Referring organisation
NEW LYMINGE SURGERY

Booking reference number
[redacted]

You'll notice the reference to June 10th, just under a month from the day I received that text. The thought that I might have to wait that long for someone to arrange an appointment (which is not, of course, the same thing as having the appointment itself), had filled me with dread. As it turns out, Cherith and I were right to be concerned. My community heart nurse recently told me that the average waiting time for an echocardiogram in our area is a year. I am pretty sure I would have been dead if it had taken that long.

But now, here it was.

The elusive machine.

The one that would tell us what was wrong with my heart.

The one that would provide a key to my treatment.

The two nurses operating this portable miracle were very cheerful characters. A lot of chat followed as they started what turned out to be a thirty-minute examination. There were moments of banter as they examined the chambers and valves of my heart, using a handheld scanner, watching as its soundwaves created video pictures on the screen. It was a thoroughly relaxing exercise.

Until, that is, near the end.

Twenty-five minutes in, the joviality ceased.

They disengaged from their conversation with Cherith and me. Their expressions changed. They started pointing to the screen and talking in a hushed tone to each other. Something was quite obviously wrong. Cherith held my hand.

"We're going to take these results and show them to the cardiologist," they said as they prepared to leave. "The heart doctor will tell you what they show."

It was clear we were going to have to wait.

Neither of us liked that very much.

Never one to enjoy being out of the loop, Cherith turned to me. "What do you think they saw?"

There was no time to confess my ignorance. The nurse looking after me – a wonderful woman called Monica – had found me a bed to replace the gurney. Yes, a hospital bed! This was the fourth piece of high-tech equipment of the day. So far, I had seen a cardiac monitor, a blood test ultrasound, and an echocardiogram. Now it was an electric bed. And what a relief that was. For those of you unfamiliar with the modern hospital bed, it is equipped with switches on both sides which can control the height of the mattress from the ground and the elevation of the head of the bed, creating the perfect incline for someone like me who needed to be almost upright if they were to have any chance of easing the pressure on their chest. It's an expensive piece of kit. No wonder there's such a shortage of them.

For the rest of the day, I slipped in and out of sleep while Cherith sat beside me. She was in no hurry to go home; our small house was being redecorated, so everything was in turmoil, including our bedroom. When the time eventually came to say goodbye, neither of us gave voice to the one question that was on both our lips.

What had the nurses seen on the echocardiogram?

DAY 3
WEDNESDAY

MAY 15TH 2024

And there was evening, and there was morning - the third day.

Genesis 1:13

CHAPTER 8

THE DARKEST HOURS

Just one hour after Cherith had left for home – a car journey of about twenty-five minutes – it was all change once again. The space I had been occupying in the Rapid Assessment Ward was needed for a more acute patient, so a porter arrived to take me to a new destination. When I arrived at a new ward, I could see that it was much more modern than the ones I had been used to so far. It seemed to function as some kind of interim ward between Rapid Assessment and the wards where patients were most likely to spend most of their stay. Impressed by the shiny new surroundings in my side room, I took a few sneaky photos on my phone and sent them via WhatsApp to Cherith. It was now about 10.30pm. I had already been to the toilet before leaving Rapid Assessment, so I found the most comfortable position in my electric bed and closed my eyes. My side room had a proper door rather than just a curtain. Maybe I was going to sleep at last.

This was not to be. My first problem was the cardiac

monitor next to me. The alarm on this machine seemed to be even louder than the one in Rapid Assessment. It also seemed to go off far more frequently. I used the red button to ask for a nurse to see if she could reduce the noise so I could stand a chance of sleeping. I had not managed a proper sleep since arriving at the hospital. If truth be told, I hadn't enjoyed a full night's sleep for a very long time. She did her best to adjust the settings, but her efforts made little difference. In any case, even my eyes could see that my heart was not functioning. The readings on the screen kept dropping to levels which triggered the loud beeping sounds to alert the nurses at the central reservation in the corridor outside my room. I was going to have to make the best of a bad situation.

The second problem turned out to be a whole lot more serious. At about 3.00am, a nurse came into my room.

"You haven't urinated since getting here," she said. It sounded like a statement of fact but the uplift in tone at the end of the sentence signalled it was a question.

"I went before I left Rapid Assessment," I answered.

"In that case, I'm going to have to fit a catheter."

Looking back, I now realise that I was the one that should have been asking a question. Why did I need a catheter? I had been peeing voluminously the previous day, and the evening too. The effects of the diuretic injection had seen to that, but by the time I arrived at this new room the effects had subsided, hence my lack of any need to use a portable male urinal, or the toilet. In retrospect, I should have questioned this, or at least asked questions about why the catheter was necessary, how long it would be needed for, and what benefits it would be adding, but I was so exhausted –

spaced out even – that I didn't have the capacity to pause the process.

The nurse opened some packets and spread the contents over the table next to my bed. I could see a large syringe, a plastic tube, a transparent bag, and some other objects. It didn't take any high degree of imaginative effort on my part to predict what some of these devices might be used for, or where they might be ending up on my body. When the nurse left the room for what she said would be "a few moments" – but which turned out to be half an hour - I was left anticipating my fate and wondering how much it was going to hurt.

It was going to hurt a lot.

Even if you're not a bloke, you can, I'm sure, imagine something of the pain involved in having a tube inserted into that part of the male anatomy. Even with the poor excuse for an anaesthetic – a kind of analgesic liquid of some kind – the sensation was enough to make me gasp, groan, and shout. The insertion was far further and deeper than I imagined it would be. When it was at last in place, I expected to utter a deep sigh of relief, but the truth is I felt bruised. From that second on, every time I moved the lower part of my body, I had an indescribable sensation of pain. Even shifting a millimetre caused a sudden pang. There was no chance of feeling comfortable.

When the nurse left, I tried to sleep, but the insistent and persistent clamour of the cardiac monitor and my unrelenting nervousness about moving my body to get comfortable combined to create a perfect storm of restlessness. As the night wore on, I became more and more deflated. I had filled the catheter bag to about one quarter of its capacity very soon after it was fitted, but it had seemed to stop at that point. When the need to pee arose, nothing appeared to be passing through to the bag. I thought this was normal, so I said nothing. I had allowed myself to become passive, stripped of all normal agency. Today, I know I should have acted.

At about 4.00am, a porter entered and off we went along low-lit and deserted corridors. He was a friendly man in his fifties called Terry. His father had been a hospital porter too. When the subject of his pay came up, I couldn't believe what a paltry sum it was. This feller was doing something that 99% of the people I know wouldn't even dream of doing. I include myself in that percentage. The hours are insane, the wear and tear horrible. Terry told me he had injured his back lifting one patient. He had been three weeks in agony and still wasn't back to full fitness. This was one of a few moments during my stay in hospital when I became livid – or as livid as my sick heart would permit – at the indifference and incompetence of successive governments in their treatment of the NHS in general, and of its frontline staff in particular. Clapping them every Thursday night during the pandemic was nice enough as affirmation goes, but what they really needed then – and need now - was better practical support, including improved staff numbers and fairer, better salaries. During those minutes being looked after by Terry, the rage was greater than the pain.

As we neared our destination, I asked Terry whether he enjoyed doing his job.

"Love it," he replied.

"But why?"

"Meeting people like you. I love having conversations. It

makes it all worthwhile."

As he wheeled me through the doors to my new 'home' – the Cardiac Care Unit – I remember the amazement and admiration I felt for this man. As he handed me over to the care of a nurse, I told him how grateful I was for what he had done for me. He nodded, smiled, then made his way out of the double doors into the corridor, heading to the next person he was asked to ferry.

As dawn approached, the pain caused by the catheter intensified. At this point, you are probably asking why I didn't complain to the nursing staff and get the matter sorted. The truth is that I have a place I go to in my head when I'm experiencing grave discomfort of either a physical or emotional kind. I developed this dissociative state when I was very young. On my eighth birthday, I was sent away to a boarding school – Cheam School, the same place King Charles III went when he was little. It was run by a sadistic headmaster who beat me savagely on my first day (what an unforgettable birthday present) and three subsequent occasions during my first fortnight. Later in my time at Cheam I was abused sexually by a member of staff. In all these situations, I learned to dissociate. As I've written elsewhere, if a child can't escape in their body they will learn to escape in their minds. That's what I did as a child when experiencing pain. It's a state that allows you to fly away in your imagination while still being in your body.

That was the psychological state I now entered as dawn greeted the Cardiac Care Unit at the William Harvey Hospital in Ashford. Looking back at my WhatsApp messages that morning, I can tell I was in this survival mode because I only had enough energy to write a text to Cherith with the name of the new ward. Nothing else. None of the normal acts of communication. No tokens of affection. I had enough energy to write an address, but that's all. I had entered a state of dissociation that I had learned as a little boy. It had not been a matter of conscious choice. More an instinctive reflex.

By the time Cherith arrived around 9.30am, I was in a very dark space in a poorly lit ward. I had not managed to add anything to my catheter bag in hours. I was desperate to wee and in immense pain. When my nurse – a woman called Yumi – came to give me my injections, I was too distressed to ask for help.

What made matters worse was the state of the veins in my arms. They just weren't showing at all that morning, so it took a while for Yumi to fit me with a new cannula. To be honest, even Blood Test Man – the guy with the portable ultrasound – would have had a job that morning, so this is no criticism of Yumi at all. She took a while to locate a cooperative vein, but when she did, she managed to secure the cannula and inject the medication I needed.

Including the diuretic.

Within the hour, this began to make life unbearable. By now I was connected to a telemetry box that hung around my neck, not to a bedside monitor. Somehow, I shuffled with Cherith's help to the toilet next to the nurse's station. I entered the room and pulled down my pyjama trousers. By this time, I was almost delirious with pain. Without thinking about the consequences, I pulled at the tube connecting my bruised penis to the catheter bag.

I cannot, and perhaps should not, describe the feeling.

All I'll say is that I screamed.

One name.

Yumi.

She came running into the toilet.

She took one look at me, assessed the situation, and said, "Don't touch anything! Just wait until I come back."

Yumi returned within seconds carrying the required equipment to disassemble the catheter, including a local anaesthetic. Within a further few seconds, the awful instrument of torture was mercifully removed, and I was dashing to the toilet. There, to quote an apocalyptic Scripture, I heard the welcome sound of many rushing waters. The relief was unimaginable. When I flushed the toilet, I saw to my horror that there was blood in the water.

Yumi and Cherith got me back to the bed where I lay down on my back, amazed at the freedom I felt below, the lack of wincing torment at even the tiniest movements of my lower body. Meanwhile, I heard one of the staff call out that there was "blood on the floor" in the room I'd just left. I had obviously not made it to the toilet without an accident. Some kind soul went in to clean up the mess I had made.

A little while later, a doctor dressed in a suit arrived. He introduced himself as a cardiologist. He had been talking to the other patients on the ward, all of whom were seriously ill with various heart conditions. When he came and sat with me, all I heard was snippets of information, all delivered in a professional, low-key voice.

Some parts were practical.

"You'll be here ten days."

"You'll be taken next week to the Royal Brompton Hospital to have an MRI done on your heart."

Other parts were technical.

"Dilated cardiomyopathy."

"First degree heart block."

"Implant."

"In the event of a fatal arrhythmia."

When he had finished sharing, he turned to me and asked, "Do you have any cardiac history in your family?"

"I was adopted," I explained. "I don't know anything about the medical records of my parents."

According to Cherith, I then shared that I had been under immense stress because I had been a victim of criminal abuse, and the Church had covered it up. I had been interviewed about this a lot on the news, and it had all taken its toll. I said that I had been a priest but had now resigned. Cherith says I broke down at this point.

When he left, I was beyond exhausted. Cherith says that I was out of it on and off for the rest of that morning and into the afternoon. She, meanwhile, was going through her own version of hell. Our loved ones go through their own trauma when they see us in pain. It would be a while before she told me exactly what she experienced during those long dark hours that Wednesday.

CHAPTER 9

ARE YOU ALRIGHT?

It would only be after I was back home that I would learn how Cherith had latched onto the word "fatal" during the doctor's visit to my bedside that day. She had already concluded that I might not be long for this world. I had looked a mixture of ghostly and ghastly when she entered the Cardiac Care Unit earlier that morning. The whole atmosphere and tone of the ward was dark. The other patients looked so much more seriously ill than those on the Rapid Assessment Ward and at A&E during the previous days. When the heart doctor had mentioned the fact that I might suffer a *fatal* arrhythmia, even though it was an entirely hypothetical statement – one delivered in a clinical voice – she had received the information in a very different spirit from the one intended. She interpreted it as a death sentence.

"Are you alright?" she asked me.

"I'm doing okay."

"Are you sure you're alright?"

"Yes."

"You would tell me if you didn't feel alright?"

I nodded and grunted.

"Darling, I need to know if you're not. You will tell me, won't you? Please promise me."

"Yes."

"Yes, you're alright, or yes you promise?"

"Both."

"So, you're alright?"

I closed my eyes and sighed.

At this point, Cherith realised her approach was not conducive to me resting so she left the ward to have what she has since described to me as "a wee reset". She went down to the café, bought herself a coffee, and did what most daughters do under testing circumstances. She phoned her mother back home.

Cherith's mother and father are Northern Irish. They are religious people in the Ian Paisley mould - Protestant, evangelical, dogmatic, and sometimes strident. They can be firm and stern when they want to be. They are also some of the kindest and most caring people you could ever hope to meet, full of human compassion, ready to help in any way they can. They are wonderfully supportive to Cherith, and indeed to me. We are very, very blessed.

"Mum, it's really serious," Cherith said. She followed this with, "I'm really scared I'm going to lose him."

"Let's just look at the facts," Mum said, her voice strong and calm. "What have they actually said?"

Cherith started to relay the information given by the heart doctor a little while before. When she mentioned the word "implant," her mother asked her if he had explained what that was.

"A pacemaker," Cherith said. Then she added, "He also mentioned an internal defibrillator."

"That doesn't sound too bad. Lots of people have those and they lead perfectly normal lives."

Cherith began to feel more reassured.

"I think I might be annoying Mark," she said. There was a note of contrition in her voice.

"What do you mean?"

"I kept asking if he was alright just now. I don't think I was being very helpful."

"Ach now, Cherith. I don't suppose he'd appreciate that. Perhaps that's not the best thing."

Cherith agreed.

"I'm due to meet a friend," her mother said. "Do you want me to cancel so I can be here for you?"

99 times out of 100, Cherith would have said no, but this time she needed her mother.

"Phone me if you need to," her Ma concluded.

A short while later, as Cherith sipped her coffee downstairs, a text came through from her mother on WhatsApp. There were two statements that stood out in her comments. The first was about the pacemaker prospect. "We have heard of a few people who've had pacemakers recently." The second was more devotional. And "Little thing has just come up this moment on my phone. 'You are not alone. God is with you.' Hold hard to that Cherith – not just a nice wee saying." That was religious, yes, but it was comforting.

You may be thinking that I have more than a bit of religion myself, having been a vicar. The truth is I have struggled in recent years when it comes to the world of organised religion. I was abused in the late 70s and early 80s by an evangelical barrister and acting judge by the name of John Smyth QC. He was Mary Whitehouse's lawyer and an ardent anti-gay campaigner, well known for his forthright views in the UK. The BBC even ran a dramatic reconstruction of the gay news trial in which my abuser was played by a well-known actor. What no one knew at the time was that Smyth was physically and spiritually abusing boys and young men at my school and later at my university. He caused lifelong harm to those of us he groomed and victimised.

In 2017, Cathy Newman of Channel 4 News approached me and asked if I would speak to her on camera about these abuses, and the coverup of these horrors by senior Church of England figures in the 80s and more recently – a coverup that goes right to the top of this ancient Christian institution. I agreed, and this led to what is now seven years of campaigning. At one point, when justice at last looked likely – when the Crown Prosecution Service had said that the evidentiary threshold had been crossed – my abuser died of complications after a relatively routine heart procedure out in South Africa.

After this, my fellow survivors and I pushed for an independent investigation into the Smyth abuses and the church's response, or lack of it. The Church of England agreed to commission an independent review. By May 2024, the publication of that review was four years late. The frustration suffered by many of Smyth's victims felt like a further abuse on top of the original ones inflicted by Smyth himself. We had to confront and endure a lot of denial, deflection, distancing, and outright duplicity from senior clergy within the church. These men and women showed time after time that they were far more concerned about protecting the tribe than the traumatised. They failed to understand that silence is a form of violence.

Perhaps you can understand now why this ex-vicar has a problem or two with organised religion, why in fact I came to the place where I felt I had no choice but to resign altogether from the Church of England in the months running up to suffering from heart failure. My heart had simply had enough of what I saw as a toxic cocktail of incompetence and corruption. But my heart had not had enough of God. My heart still possesses a love for God, a need for God, a belief in God, it's just that I am not a churchman anymore. I'm not a company man – a person who supports an institution. I believe that God exists. I believe that God is the Love of all loves. I believe that God is supremely the perfect embodiment and expression of kindness – that God is the exact opposite of the kind of angry and vengeful Being promoted by Smyth. Jesus asked us to call God "our Father", and in my mind, God is like the dad who adopted me in 1961 – someone slow to anger and abounding in love; someone who focuses on the precious in us not the worthless; someone who loves us more than the best of human beings ever could. I have never wavered in that faith. I hope I never will.

When I was rushed into hospital, all I can say is that I felt carried by this divine kindness. At the risk of sounding a little rude, at no point did I want to be visited by an ordained minister from some church denomination. At no point did I want a service around my bed. I just wanted to rest in the arms of this everlasting love.

A few days after her chat with her mother, when Cherith was asked by her work colleagues how she was doing, she answered with these very simple but powerful words: "I feel held and upheld by other people's prayers." Her friends and colleagues seemed to know what that meant. One of them even had tears in her eyes.

This feeling of being held and upheld by other's prayers was something very real for me too. If I'm honest, I was much too weak to do any praying myself. Apart from a few wordless sighs for divine help – especially that morning in the toilet - I had no resources to even form the thoughts that might turn into prayer. What I experienced instead was the knowledge that other people who cared about us were praying, and this helped more than words could ever express.

Even more humbling was hearing that complete strangers were praying for us, and from the other side of the world. My twin sister Claire lives in Utah with her husband Jeff and my beloved nephew Jamie. As soon as she heard what was happening to me, Claire got church friends praying. Some of these were in Utah, but many were in the city and state from which she had moved – Albuquerque, New Mexico. In the message you're about to read, Claire calls me 'Starkers'. This is because when we were little, if it was a very hot day, I would run stark naked through the sprinklers as they shot jets of cooling water in the air to give the thirsty soil a good drink. Staire is my nickname for her. Cheery is my nickname for Cherith, who is nearly always cheerful.

15 May 2024

Starkers I've asked my small prayer group to pray for you. So now you're being showered with the very best from these faithful prayer warriors. Peace and love from us all here in Utah and Albuquerque 🩶 20:55

Ah that's just wonderful. Thank you so so much. I'm ending the day much better than I started, feeling better generally. So much of this is down to prayer. Thank you Staire for yours and for those of this very kind group of yours. Truly. Cheery has just left to go home and I'm now tucking myself up in a ward full of old men! Characters! Love you all lots xxx 20:59

Love you too. Have a good nights rest and we'll talk tomorrow. Xxxx 21:00

At the risk of sounding a little mystical, the effect of all this praying was that I became aware of an enveloping peace during the entire course of my week in hospital. This peace, which I believe is an effect of the divine love, or more specifically Jesus, was so reassuring that at no point did I sense any fear at all. There is a sacred text that tells us that perfect love drives out fear (1 John 4:18). That's my story too. The serenity of another world calmed my heart, keeping it from surrendering to anxiety or despair. Like Cherith, I was being upheld. I just knew that my loving heavenly Father was right there with me, holding and enfolding me in his strong and healing embrace.

Although I was too ill to read the Bible, I did have some verses in my mind during the week - a passage in the writings of the prophet Isaiah (Isaiah 43:2).

> When you pass through the waters,
> I will be with you;
> and when you pass through the rivers,
> they will not sweep over you.
> When you walk through the fire,
> you will not be burned;
> the flames will not set you ablaze.

The first thought that struck me was that this passage does not say "if" you pass through water and fire. It says "when." The promise isn't one of prevention. It's one of presence. Whenever we go through waters, through rivers, through the fire, we will be aware of God's presence. That was my testimony in hospital.

The second thought that struck me had to do with the word "through". The promise is not that we will be guided *around* our difficulties. It is that we will be accompanied *through* them. Our Father may be in heaven, as the Lord's Prayer puts it, but his hand will hold our hand whenever we pass through rough seas or raging fires here on earth. That was also my testimony.

As human beings, we are so pain averse that we tend to construct religious beliefs that promise people we will not have to go through suffering. But Isaiah didn't promise prevention. He promised presence. He promised, "I will be with you."

As Cherith's mother remained available to her beloved daughter during those darkest hours, the light began to shine. It came in the form of a WhatsApp message that her mother sent during the day – a text in which she had felt prompted to pass on something that had stood the test of time and comforted countless people for over 2500 years. Here's a screenshot of her message.

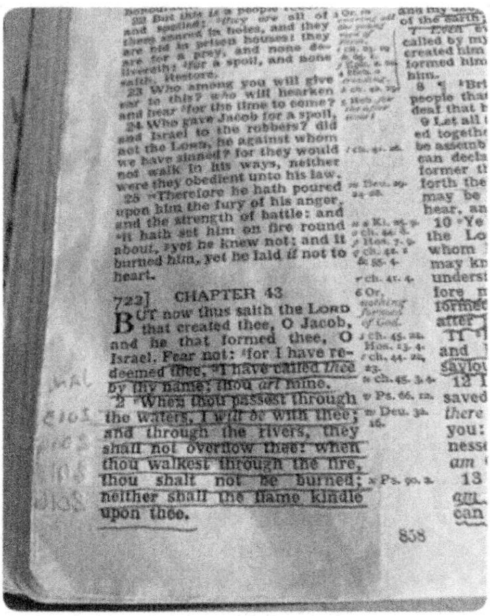

Cherith I want you to read these underlined words to Mark at some point. They are very comforting and encouraging. Of course he will know them very well. xxxx

14:37

I can't tell you how buoyed I felt by this.

Cherith's Mum was focused on the same passage.

When Cherith came back to the Cardiac Care Unit after lunch, the ward seemed lighter. I had managed to get some sleep, and she had managed to have her reset. She didn't need to ask if I was alright any more than I needed to ask. We both knew.

My reassuring nurse, Yumi, came and shared that I would soon be moved to St Batholomew – a nearby cardiac ward. This for me was the final assurance I needed. I had never heard of the ward, but I had heard of Bartholemew. He is thought to have been the same person as Nathaniel, a figure mentioned in the early pages of the Gospel of John. When Jesus meets Nathaniel, he takes one look at him and declares, "this is a man with no bad thing in his heart." While I appreciate that 'heart' denoted something moral rather than medical in the Bible, I still felt uplifted by the mention of Bartholomew..

One of the things Jesus was noted for was his knowledge of the human heart. It was said of him that he did not need to hear a testimonial about another person because he could monitor what was in their heart just by looking at them. The ancients had a word for this gift – *cardiognosis* in Greek. *Cardio* means "heart" and *gnosis* means "knowledge." Jesus possessed a deep understanding of other peoples' hearts. He could diagnose their spiritual condition with just one look. In this respect, Jesus of Nazareth was the greatest heart doctor – in a moral sense – the world has ever seen. In both a physical and a spiritual sense, he was a walking echocardiogram.

And look at how he does the exact opposite of so much

toxic religion – he praises the precious in Nathaniel, he does not rail against the worthless. In praising the positive, he reveals himself as the knower of hearts (*cardiognostes*), and Nathaniel is the grateful beneficiary. What a providential touch it was to be going to a ward named after a saint with a good heart!

After all these tokens of otherworldly reassurance, Cherith and I knew that we were passing through a fiery ordeal, yes, but we also knew that we were in the company of a luminous and numinous love, and that made everything, well, alright.

As the day ended, I received a message from young Jamie, my wonderful young nephew, in Utah. It filled me with great warmth and hope then, and it is doing the same now.

CHAPTER 10

A CASE OF DEJA VU

The moment I was wheeled into St Bartholemew, I felt different. The sun seemed to reach every corner of the room through the windows and the whole atmosphere felt so much lighter and brighter. I was welcomed by a nurse called Abi who was to look after me with undiminished cheerfulness and genuine compassion for the next five days. She set to work as soon as I was settled.

I had been separated from my telemetry box just before leaving the Cardiac Care Unit. This was a device about the size of a hardback fiction book that hung around my neck. The leads attached to my body had been connected to this box, recording and transmitting my vital signs to the nurse's station at the previous ward. On leaving the Cardiac Care Unit, I had taken the box off and handed it back to Yumi. On entering Saint Bartholemew, I needed a new one.

After an hour, Cherith tapped my arm.

"Shouldn't they have connected you by now?"

"Oh no. I'm sure it's alright. Abi's got lots to do. She'll be here in no time. Don't worry about it."

Cherith *was* worrying, however. She was quite rightly thinking that even though the nurses in the hospital performed miracles, none of them could be expected to know my heartrate or heartbeat by some kind of mystical intuition. The box was needed.

"I'm just popping to the loo," she said.

I took her at her word. What she was in fact doing was going to the nurse's station, finding Abi, and asking her if I was supposed to be connected to a monitoring device.

"Thank you for reminding me," Abi said.

When Abi returned, she put fresh electrodes and stickers on my chest and restored the connection to the telemetry box. As she left the bay and closed the curtain, she smiled at Cherith who smiled back at her. I would only find out what that smile was all about while walking the dogs with Cherith four months later!

Under Abi's expert and compassionate care, and the care of all the other phenomenal staff on duty at St Bartholomew, I began to sense a new determination to push through during that afternoon. Cherith sat by my side until 9pm, taking in the surroundings as I was. I was in a men's ward with four others. Opposite me on the right was a man in his sixties called Joe. He was a lorry driver from Leicester who'd had a heart attack in his cab a few days before and been rushed into hospital. His wife was a good three hours away and unable to see him. Over the next four days, I didn't see him receive a single visitor. One thing he said really struck me. He had experienced several episodes of extreme breathlessness in the months prior to his shock.

"I wish I'd paid more attention to those."

Joe was six months or so from retirement, so the heart attack had ruined his plans. His lorry had been driven back to the depot in Leicester, and he was now desperate to return not only to his wife but to work. But the body heals at its own speed. Although we can aid the healing process with our attitudes and actions, we are not in charge of the process and it's the medical experts who determine when we are ready to leave, not us. Joe was impatient to leave, but he had to wait. In the end, I would leave before him.

Directly opposite me was a gentle soul called Terry. Over 90 years old, Terry had suffered a heart attack and was clearly struggling. He was also lonely. A young couple would visit him on Saturday evening, but that was it. So, Cherith and I started to get to know him. It turned out that Terry had spent all his working life in the merchant navy and been on some interesting vessels to some equally interesting places. His wife had died quite recently. His only child – a daughter – had died of cancer in her forties. It was obvious from his furrowed face and vulnerable eyes that he had endured a lot. My failing heart went out to him. He was a proper, Kentish gentleman.

Opposite me to my left was Alan, whom I called Big Al, because he was tall and well-built. Cherith and I agree to this day that we have never seen a fitter looking octogenarian. He was 85, but he looked 65. Yet, he too had suffered a serious heart attack. The previous Sunday, he had been out walking early in the morning around Radnor Park in our neighbouring town of Folkestone. He had felt severe chest pain and fallen on the pavement. Somehow, he dragged himself to the entrance of the Royal Victoria Hospital nearby in the park. The staff gave him emergency care and he was rushed to the hospital in Ashford, where he ended up in Saint Bartholemew.

On my left, separated by a drawn curtain, was a man of similar age to Big Al, although this gentleman, who I quickly learned was called Rupert, had a voice that we would all associate with upstairs at Downton Abbey. Cherith says that I can sound posh sometimes, but I'm nowhere near as upper-class as Rupert. Rupert was with his wife Cordelia, who sounded like a member of the royal household.

I'll give you a flavour of Rupert's personality. I think many of you will recognise it without too much trouble or time. Cherith became fascinated by the conversations in the next-door bay. She is excellent at both short-term memorization and humorous impersonations. She wrote down one part of what our new neighbours were saying and sent it in a message to her mother.

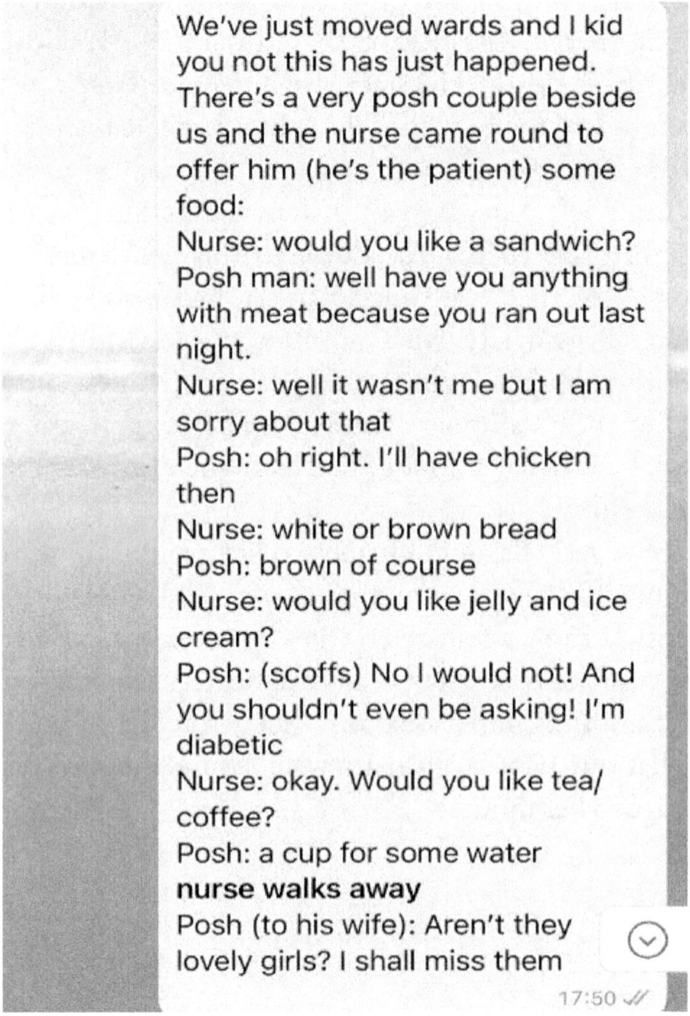
We've just moved wards and I kid you not this has just happened. There's a very posh couple beside us and the nurse came round to offer him (he's the patient) some food:
Nurse: would you like a sandwich?
Posh man: well have you anything with meat because you ran out last night.
Nurse: well it wasn't me but I am sorry about that
Posh: oh right. I'll have chicken then
Nurse: white or brown bread
Posh: brown of course
Nurse: would you like jelly and ice cream?
Posh: (scoffs) No I would not! And you shouldn't even be asking! I'm diabetic
Nurse: okay. Would you like tea/ coffee?
Posh: a cup for some water
nurse walks away
Posh (to his wife): Aren't they lovely girls? I shall miss them
17:50

A little while later, when everything was quiet in the ward, Rupert and Cordelia started doing a crossword. That was undeniably cute, but the execution of it was not. Rupert seemed to be one of those husbands who had to be right all the time. This at one point caused him to crowbar a German word into an English crossword – a word that clearly wasn't meant to be there, and which unsurprisingly created havoc in the crossword itself. All this was much to Cordelia's frustration, although she kept her impatience in check, restricting herself to gentle complaints rather than harsh reprimands. Everyone listening to this was doing their best to behave. Cherith and I, being new to the ward, were perhaps the least successful. Some of the others showed more deference; I had already noticed signs of cap-doffing towards Rupert.

I am sure some of you may think less of me for noting all this, but you must remember that by profession I am a writer, especially of novels, and that I spend much of my life engaged in what some refer to as people watching. Some of my characters are based on real people and remembered conversations. I'm unable to pass by any golden opportunities to record human eccentricity. Adversity can be a very special source of creativity, and in my case the fun involved can be a way of coping with the harsher moments of life. And coping is what I had been doing for the last three days.

And coping is where I may have had something of an advantage. I have always seen my ten years away at boarding school as a disadvantage in terms of my emotional growth. Being exiled to a strange country house on my eighth birthday was not something that washed over me like water over a duck's back. I hated it. It felt like abandonment which, of course, it was. That, and the abuses I suffered both at my prep school and my public school, caused lifelong harm. That legacy cannot be regarded as anything but detrimental.

But it wasn't completely destructive. There were the English teachers whose influence gave me a love for literature and a longing to write for a living. There were the sporting opportunities which allowed me to excel at soccer in the school's first XI where I dressed like, and tried to impersonate, Norwich City's most famous goalkeeper – Kevin Keelan – as I hurled myself through the air in my green top, green shorts, and mustard-yellow socks (more of this in a few chapters). I will always be grateful for those academic and footballing privileges, even if the emotional cost of my school years was great.

And there was one more thing.

Sleeping in dormitories.

I remember talking to my adoptive father, Philip Stibbe, about his experiences as a POW. He had been in Wingate's Army and wounded in action. He was taken to Rangoon jail where he spent several years as a prisoner, facing extreme challenges.

"How did you cope?" I asked Dad one day.

"Boarding school was a good preparation."

"What do you mean?"

"I mean, the strictly observed timetabled routine, the beatings, the sleeping in what immediately resembled a male dormitory. I had seen a version of all this before."

I understood immediately what he meant. About eight years after this conversation, I was the vicar of a church in Hertfordshire. I invited Jonathan Aitken to speak at one of our Sunday services. He had been a member of parliament, broken the law, and been sent to prison. During his talk in church, he said something that sounded just like what my father had shared about Rangoon jail.

"People often ask me how I coped with prison. I answer, boarding school. It felt just the same. That made it easier."

When Cherith left the ward at 9pm, I lay down on the

electric bed and looked at my new surroundings. Adaptation came easily and swiftly to me that night. Somewhere in the recesses of my mind, Saint Bartholemew turned into a boarding school dormitory. The nurses morphed into the matrons I had known at school. The occasional alarms turned into the clanging of boarding house bells. The other men in the ward underwent a Benjamin Button-like metamorphosis and became the kind of boys among whom I had once slept when I was young. Switching off the lights at 10.00pm reprised the familiar marking of the end of every day at school known as 'lights out'. That's how I managed to cope, through sensing the resonances from a bygone time. In that sense, boarding school had done something positive for me. It gave me some lifelong keys to resilience. Lying in the ward, it was as if I was hearing an old and familiar tune.

The day had started with excruciating pain and feelings of dark desperation in the toilet of the Cardiac Care Unit. Now it was ending in the warm and quiet surroundings of a new ward. The intense and bloody discomfort seemed like a distant memory, and the gun-metal colour of despair was now replaced by a vibrant yellow hue called hope. In my repairing heart, it was like seeing the first daffodils of Spring on a walk with our dogs.

DAY 4
THURSDAY

MAY 16TH 2024

And there was evening, and there was morning - the fourth day.

Genesis 1:19

CHAPTER 11

AN ANGEL IN SCRUBS

The next day, Thursday, something truly remarkable happened – an occurrence that some will attribute to providence, others to a chance coincidence. To appreciate the full significance of what I'm about to share, I need to take you back in time to November 2018, three weeks after Cherith and I had moved into our tiny rented home in the Garden of England, the fine county of Kent.

The village that became our new community is situated between the East Kent Downs and the English Channel. On a good day you can see beyond Folkestone to the coast of France. Our village boasts a pub that's been unchanged since World War 2, and a 12th century chapel named after a Celtic saint. The church stands in the middle of a field, surrounded by grazing sheep and horses. We are said to have the fewest people and the tallest steeple in the county.

Shortly after arriving, the landlord of our property sent me an email inviting us to the next parish council meeting in the pub. He doubted if the topics would interest us, but he added that because I was a novelist, I might find some of the council members interesting. They might even provide the inspiration for a book.

Cherith and I arrived at the pub for the meeting. Most of the people present were north of 70. One chap who was without doubt in that age range, seeing how young Cherith was, asked, "Are you pregnant?" A ripple of nervous laughter spread across the room. It wasn't exactly the most politically correct question. Fortunately for him, my Northern Irish wife is not easily offended, so she calmly replied in the negative. The reason for his question was not lost on either of us. The population of the parish stood at 39. Our arrival had upped it to 41. Clearly the interrogator hoped that we might offer the possibility of increasing it even more. Our landlord Antony was not wrong. I was already seeing the potential for a future book.

Things only got worse from here on - or better, depending on your point of view. The parish's accounts had been home to approximately £1600 for a considerable length of time. I'm talking years. Possibly even ten years. The committee had never managed to agree on a productive use of these funds. Until tonight.

A woman with fair hair, younger than the majority, though older than Cherith, proposed a use for the money. She suggested that it should be used to pay for a defibrillator. This, she contended, should be placed outside the same pub in which we were all sitting, that it should have a code, that this code should be shared with the council members, and that it should be used to save the life of anyone who had overdone it at the bar and suffered from a heart attack. This seemed to me to be a very wise and justifiable use of the stagnant funds.

As she spoke, I couldn't help noticing how dogged and determined this woman was. There was a hint of a Scandinavian accent in her voice. Like a true Viking, she wasn't going to accept defeat, even when emotions became heated (as they can do in these small English committee meetings) and people's use of language became coarse and blunt. She was going to keep fighting until she had the victory. I have done a lot of speaking in Scandinavia over many years. I have always loved the people of Norway, Sweden, and Denmark. Turns out she was Danish. I liked her immediately.

It also turned out she was a cardiologist, and her name was Dr Anne Louise Vaney. That's why she was advocating so eloquently for a defibrillator. It's also why she knew her stuff and made her case so well. I, for one, was persuaded. So was Cherith. When it came to the vote, we both said aye to her proposal. It was passed. The defibrillator was purchased. It now stands outside the pub, about two hundred yards away from where I'm sitting as I write this.

All that was fascinating and – as you can see now – fine fodder for future book writing. Thank you, Antony! But there's something else I need to share. During the meeting, as this woman was speaking, it became obvious why she was such a good cardiologist. While I listened to her championing the cause of the defibrillator, I distinctly remember thinking, "Oh God, if ever I have any serious issues with my heart, I want this woman to be my doctor." I knew that if the way she tackled these men and fought for this cause was anything to go by, I would be in the best possible hands.

That was the last time I saw her.

Until I entered hospital 5 ½ years later.

I was resting in the ward when a woman with fair hair entered. She was dressed in hospital blue.

"We've had a meeting to discuss your situation," she said. "I'm fairly sure I know what's wrong with you, and what we need to do to get you back on your feet again."

Her tone was strong.

Reassuring.

"The two chambers of your heart are not in sync. That's why you've got such an unusual and irregular heart rhythm. We need to insert a device into your chest that will fix the problem. It's a turbo unit. State of the art. Latest model. It will have two functions. The first is to sync the two chambers and create a regular rhythm. The second is a kind of backup. If you have a fatal arrhythmia, it will kickstart your heart again, so you'll basically be resuscitated. Think of that second function as a kind of internal, personal defibrillator."

"How does it work?" Cherith asked.

"The unit we're going to put in your chest will have three electric leads. Two of these will connect with the two chambers of your heart. The third will connect with another part of your heart. The heart is really an electric pump. Yours has not been working efficiently. It's been operating at about 25%. These leads, along with your medication, will increase the percentage and get things working better."

"You said you were fairly sure this was the solution," I said. "You didn't say you were completely sure."

"No, that's right. We are going to send you off for an angiogram this afternoon. We need to know that the arteries around your heart are all clear. If they are, then the solution I've just described to you will be the right way forward."

Cherith and I looked at each other and nodded. This was the first time anyone had explained clearly and in layman's terms what was wrong with me and what needed to happen.

The woman in the lightweight scrubs looked at me and smiled. "By the way, we're neighbours. I live in the same village!"

Suddenly, the lights went on in my head, and in Cherith's too. This was the woman who had fought for the defibrillator at our local pub. This was the woman who was fighting for another one – mine - in the William Harvey Hospital. This was the person that over five years ago I had prayed would help me if ever I needed someone to get my heart working properly again. It all made sense now. That's why she had a slight Scandinavian accent.

After Dr Vaney had gone, Cherith texted her mother straight away, saying that this woman's name had been in her phone all along. "I'm blown away by God's kindness. Speechless," she wrote. Her mother replied, "He is the God of many surprises!"

It is hard to put into words the change in our mental state after Dr Anne Louise departed. She left clarity in her wake, which was priceless, but she also left positivity. Cherith and I had been in a dark and bleak place, but after the visit of our expert interventionist cardiologist we felt so much brighter and more hopeful. The whole journey now seemed to be one that we were not taking on our own. Someone seemed to be watching over us. Something far greater than ourselves was working on our behalf. It felt unmistakable.

It's worth pausing and thinking a bit more about this. I

have a new friend called Dr Naomi Murphy who is a trauma therapist. She is smart and articulate. When I told her about some of my hospital experiences, she commented that she had grown up with a religious faith but would now describe herself as no longer committed or active in that world. For her, the best word to describe what had happened to me was not God but "synchronicity." If you've read Carl Jung's later works, you'll be familiar with this concept.

Synchronicity is a combination of two Greek words – *syn*, meaning with, and *chronos*, meaning time. Synchronicity signifies the coming together of two events that appear to have a meaningful connection. Some regard these as *acausal*. In other words, they believe these events are not the result of any higher power – whether that higher power is God, or some paranormal reality - but the product of chance. Others, building on the findings of quantum physics – which discovered that particles are interconnected rather than separate realities – suggest that such occurrences do have meaning, and that what Lisa Miller calls "the awakened brain" can become alert to such interconnections in a way that is psycho-spiritually enriching. The awakened brain notices these synchronicities. As Carl Jung put it, "synchronicity is an ever-present reality for those who have eyes to see."

I'm not going to get into a philosophical let alone psychoanalytical argument here about what may or may not have been at work in my life during those days. I'm just going to say that while I like the word synchronicity, my preference is to tell you what I believe, which is that the strange reappearance of Dr Anne Louise Vaney was a matter of providence, and therefore not something I can justify using the language of science and reason alone. I was aware that many people were praying for me during these testing times. These prayers, I believe, were answered in varied ways, one of which was this synchronicity with Anne Louise. I think it was Archbishop William Temple who once said that when we cease praying, we cease seeing coincidences. There seems to me to be an increase in these meaningful and awe-inspiring occurrences when prayer is in the air.

During this time, our landlord Antony sent Cherith a text. He had asked people in his church to pray. One of those people was someone dear to me, a woman called Philippa.

"As I was praying for Mark, this Scripture touched my heart for him – Psalm 73:26. 'My flesh and my heart may fail, but God is the strength of my heart and my portion forever'." Who knew there was an Old Testament verse about heart failure?

God truly was the strength of my heart during these challenging days in hospital. With his love and kindness, so evident in the eyes, hands, and voices of those caring for me in hospital, I witnessed many moments that evoked wonder. There was obviously the appearance of Dr Anne Louise Vaney. But there was something else too; Antony had said I should go to the parish council meeting because it might provide ammunition for a future book.

Well, here I am.

And I'm writing this because of an angel in scrubs.

CHAPTER 12

KEVIN KEELAN'S SHORTS

I've been an ardent Canaries fan since the late 1960s. In case you don't know, the Canaries is the nickname for Norwich City Football Club, until recently under the devoted care and oversight of one of the UK's national treasures, Delia Smith, and supported by other national treasures such as Stephen Fry. I watched many games at Carrow Road throughout the late sixties, seventies, and eighties, until life took me away from my beloved county of Norfolk and my equally beloved city of Norwich. Even then I managed to see some great games. I was within a stone's throw of Justin Fashanu when he scored his goal of the season for Match of the Day (1980), and I was at Wembley when the Canaries won the League Cup Final in 1985. The best game I ever saw was against league leaders Queens Park Rangers in 1976, which Norwich won 3-2. Today, I am still a fan, even though I live in Kent.

When I was a boy, my footballing hero was the Norwich

City goalkeeper, Kevin Keelan. He went on to make nearly 700 appearances between the early 1960s and 1980 – a club record. The reason I idolised him was down to what at the time seemed like an accident. I was about 9 years old and at school. During a game of football, the goalkeeper was injured, and it was decided by the teacher that I should replace him in goal. This was just in time to face a penalty. When the opposition player ran up to take the kick, I instinctively knew he was going to place it in the top corner to my left. As he made contact, I not only saved the goal. I caught the ball. There was an audible gasp from everyone, including the teacher. I stood, clasping the ball to my chest, now puffed with pride. It was one of the best moments of my life. From that day on I was the first-choice goalkeeper and ended up playing in that position for the school's first XI for three years.

Now that I knew that I could perform well as a goalkeeper, I naturally began to watch Kevin Keelan more closely than any of the other players in the Norwich team. I was an admirer of his athletic abilities, yes, but I was also in awe of his sartorial elegance. Keelan wore a green shirt (with the yellow Canaries badge, of course, on his chest), and a strident no 1 on the back. He wore green shorts with yellow stripes down each aside, and he sported a pair of knee-length yellow socks with green stripes. I managed to find and purchase an exact replica kit, and, with the permission of my sports teacher, I wore this lurid green outfit every time I represented the school.

You may wonder what this has to do with my time in hospital being treated for heart failure many years later. Well, when the time came for my angiogram, I was wheeled from St Bartholmew into another ward. The moment my bed passed through the doors a larger-than-life man called Ivor made his presence felt.

"I hope you're not a Man Utd supporter!"

Why he said this I have no idea. I have never supported the Red Devils. There was absolutely no indication of any allegiance in what I was wearing or how I looked. Unlike Ivor, who was covered in tattoos, my skin was and is (so far, anyway) free from any images and icons of adoration, even of my wife Cherith.

"No, I'm not," I replied. "I'm a Canaries fan!"

It just so happened that it was by now late afternoon on Thursday and later that evening Norwich City were due to play the second leg in the semi-final of the EFL Championship playoffs against Leeds Utd. The first leg had ended 0-0 at Carrow Road. Even though I was poorly, I was still committed to watching the second leg on my smartphone when I returned to the ward. Ivor knew this match was due to take place, and he also knew his boss was interested.

"That's a coincidence!" he said.

"Why?"

"The doctor who's performing the angiogram is a massive Leeds Utd supporter."

My heart – which had been doing quite well thanks to Dr Anne Louise's visit earlier – began to sink. I was already a little concerned about the angiogram if I'm honest. I had heard in the past what it involved – having a cut in your arm and a thin tube (yes, another dreaded catheter) inserted into an artery into your heart, where a dye is injected into and through your blood vessels. The dye makes visible any blockages in your heart's vessels through X-Ray imaging. The thought of that had been concentrating my mind in the hours up to being wheeled into Ivor's loud and jovial care. Now the knowledge that the doctor who was to perform this procedure was rooting for the opposition that night made it all feel a little more perilous.

The banter continued until the doctor arrived. He was greeted by Ivor informing him that the patient he was about to treat was a lifelong Norwich fan. His response was very surprising.

"I supported Norwich when I was a boy," he said. "My hero was Kevin Keelan, the goalkeeper. I had a replica outfit of his which I wore when I played football. I was a goalkeeper."

I couldn't believe what I was hearing. He didn't finish there either. When he learned that we were childhood footballing ringers, he went on to describe the shorts.

"Do you remember the yellow stripes?"

I nodded.

"I had those on mine as well," I said.

What are the chances of this happening? The man performing my angiogram played in the same position as me and wore the same kit as me when he was a boy, all because he supported the same team – until that is he transferred his allegiances to Leeds Utd. That seemed like another example of, well, yes... synchronicity.

Feeling reassured that the doctor had at least some mercy for me I relaxed and waited for the procedure to begin. The wheels started turning when Dr Anne Louise entered the ward. I hadn't expected her to be present, but she had come along for the ride, wanting to check my arteries were clear so that she could then authorise the insertion of the pacemaker in my chest. In the end, the experience was a little surreal but entirely pain free. Dr Anne Louise studied the X-Ray images live and listened to the reports from the doctor and his team about what they were observing. There was some good news at last. No damage to my arteries. Dr Anne Louise now had the information she had predicted and for which she was waiting. Clear arteries were the green light for my turbo-charged pacer to be inserted.

Once I was back in the waiting area, I listened while Dr Anne Louise phoned the Queen Elizabeth the Queen Mother Hospital in Margate and insisted that I be first on the list for surgery there the following morning. Within ten minutes, she had secured me pole position and had organised for an ambulance to pick me up at 6.00am the next day (Friday). This would take me from Ashford to Margate before the rush hour began. I would have my operation under local anaesthetic at about 9.00am. I would need to be "NBM" (nil by mouth) from 6.00pm on that Thursday evening until after my op.

Ivor wheeled me back into St Bartholemew with us both singing football chants at the top of our voices. I'm not sure the other patients really appreciated me returning and singing "Here we go, here we go, here we go!" Cherith at least thought it was reassuring. The procedure couldn't have been that bad if I was in such good voice. When Ivor said goodbye, we shook hands. It was a total joy being looked after by him and indeed the others working on my heart in the angiogram ward. They all lifted my spirits.

"How did it go?" Cherith asked.

I described the weird sensation of the flexible tube going

up my arm and into my heart, and then the equally strange experience of seeing the dye doing its work and colours appearing in the arteries around my heart on the X-Ray monitor. I told her that it was not uncomfortable, just strange, and that the results had been very encouraging. I also told her how amazing Dr Anne Louise had been.

"Remember how determined she was at that council meeting five years or so ago?"

Cherith nodded.

"Well, that's how she was when she rang the hospital. She wasn't ever going to take no for an answer."

We celebrated, although we both wondered if there would be a domino effect for other people waiting for a procedure the next day, and we worried that someone who had been expecting surgery might be postponed. However, we were reassured that the patient affected was not on the "non-elective" list. A non-elective patient is someone who has a life-threatening or urgent condition and who requires immediate care. My case had been deemed non-elective, and Dr Anne Louise had expedited my surgery.

I had something to eat before the cut-off point at 6.00pm that night. I do remember it quite vividly because I asked for cheese and biscuits. When the food arrived, I was given a small plastic packet with the words DOUBLE GLOUCESTER CHEESE in capitals on the front. There was a cartoon image of a rather wide-eyed, dappled cow on the bottom right of the front of the transparent plastic packaging. I could see no markings on the wrapping to indicate where you had to tear it open to access the 20g of mild cheese waiting inside.

Cherith and I have, for a long time, been great fans not

only of the Canaries but also of a comedian called Larry David and a TV show called *Curb your Enthusiasm* – 12 series of it. Cherith thinks Larry is very like me in many ways. I'm not sure that's a compliment, although I do think there are points of comparison. For example, at the start of one episode in a very recent series Larry is in the shower trying to open one of those brand-new plastic soap dispensers. I've wrestled with these before and become quite angry with them when the brand-new plunger has proved hard to operate. In this scene, Larry – who is stark naked under the jet stream of his shower at home – gets so mad with his soap dispenser that he starts shouting and swearing at it. In the end, he bashes it against the wall of his shower cubicle and breaks the top of the container. The liquid soap pours out at last onto his hand.

When it came to opening the Double Gloucester, I can only say that I had a Larry David moment. I tried everything. I tore at every section of the small rectangular packaging with no success. I used my teeth to try and bite it open, but I made no progress. All that happened was the cheese seemed to morph into the kind of mess a toddler would produce with putty. In the end, I walked with my telemetry box around my neck out of the ward and into the reception area just beyond the double doors. There I approached the woman on duty.

"I'm sorry to bother you, but I just can't open this packet of cheese and it's driving me insane."

"Not those again," she said with a sigh and a frown. "We're always having problems. We've even written to complain to the company that makes them, but nothing's changed."

She drew a pair of scissors from a drawer and cut the packet open at the top. I thanked her, apologised again for disturbing her, then returned to my bed.

I opened the plastic packet, which was still being stubborn, then took the broken Trump-coloured cheese. I don't think I have ever tasted anything so tasteless with the word 'cheese' emblazoned on it. It was like an eraser. Rubbery in the hand. Bland in the mouth. All that effort for this. I don't think I was ever in danger that evening of not being NBM. It was a total disappointment.

And something else qualified for that description as well.

The playoff semi-final.

Leeds Utd thumped Norwich City 4-0. My team put up a very poor show and missed their opportunity to play in the final. But somehow, none of that mattered anymore. All I could think of was my angiogram doctor and our mutual fondness for Kevin Keelan's shorts. Some things are just more important in life.

Like getting your heart mended.

This time tomorrow, I thought, *I'll have a turbo-charged pacemaker and defibrillator in my chest. All the horrible symptoms I've been living with for so long will either be gone or on their way out. I'll be tired from the op, no doubt, but the chances are I'll be sleeping well for the first time in years. I'll have a state-of-the art device giving me a new chance to live life.*

When Cherith left at her usual time – 9pm – I told her, "I'll see you when I'm back here at lunchtime tomorrow." When we kissed each other goodnight, there was a tangible peace in our embrace. The next day, Friday, I knew I would be able to face whatever came my way, just as I had many times when I was a boy, standing in the rain, dressed in Kevin Keelan's bright green shorts.

DAY 5
FRIDAY

MAY 17TH 2024

And there was evening, and there was morning - the fifth day.

Genesis 1:23

CHAPTER 13

THE QUEASY PARAMEDIC

At 5.30am on Friday morning, I was awakened by Abi who administered my injections in good time for my departure. "The ambulance will be here at 6.00am," she said.

I rushed a text to Cherith reminding her that I would send her a message when I was out of surgery and had an idea when I might be back in St Bartholemew. She answered back with a question asking how I was feeling. I can't say I was nervous or apprehensive. To be perfectly honest, I had been living with serious and unpleasant symptoms for so long that all I wanted now was to be rid of them. If the drugs I was taking through my cannula – not to forget the turbo-charged pacemaker that was about to be inserted - were as effective as I had been led to believe, then I would no longer have to endure the debilitating signs of heart failure. My heart might even grow stronger, my life brighter in the process. I therefore said I was fine.

When I look back at the days leading up to the operation I

was about to have, it had not been pleasant. I was so poorly I could barely function. My health was at an all-time low and my days and nights were about surviving not thriving. The following things had been blighting my life for months and even years.

- Persistent coughing
- Breathlessness
- Sleep deprivation
- Urinary problems
- Swelling of hands, abdomen, legs, ankles
- Fatigue
- Rapid and irregular heartbeat
- Dizziness
- Unexplained weight loss
- Feelings of nausea

The mistake I made was to think of all these for far too long as separate problems. *These are just the side effects of a long hard winter,* I thought. I*n time, these will go away one by one.* I even explained some of them away; for example, the weight loss I put down to the fact that we had welcomed a new Labrador puppy into our lives (Phoebe) and the extra exercise was responsible. It was not.

The possibility that my operation that Friday morning would bring an end to all this – if not straightaway, over time – was such a comfort that there was no room for anxiety, let alone fear. That and the constant experience that I have already described of feeling held and upheld by a peace that transcends all understanding proved to be a potent combination. All week I had been enfolded by a love that was borne on the wings of many people's prayers. This had driven the fear away, as only perfect love can.

At 6.00am, this experience of being carried took a literal turn when two young men in paramedic kit – well, younger than me, i.e., in their forties – arrived to take me to the ambulance. They were exactly the lads I needed to put me at my ease – friendly, caring, genuine, strong, safe. They pushed me to a lift and then out the exit. I was met by the warm early summer air and a bright blue Kent sky. It was the first time I had been outside since Monday afternoon.

The men in green wheeled me into the back of an ambulance and set about their separate tasks. Dave sat in the front and started the drive towards Margate. Graham sat with me in the back and took my blood pressure. I had for a very long time been reluctant to let others take my BP. I always knew it was going to be high, which is why I had been taking tablets for many years. A stressful three decades (1982-2012) had left a legacy of serious hypertension – one not helped by being over three stone overweight. Those three stones had disappeared off my body like an old and baggy garment. That morning, I was not apprehensive but curious about my BP.

"What's the reading?"

"120 over 80."

"Is that good?"

"It's about perfect, I'd love it if mine was that."

At this point, I realised I was hungry. When I was young, my mother often used to give me an ice cream or sweets if I was a good boy. When I had to be treated for epilepsy at Great Ormond Street – the same hospital where she had been a ward sister in WW2 – I remember being spoiled rotten when I came home. Maybe the craving was a reflex from those years. Maybe it was simply the fact that I'd been nil by mouth for over twelve hours. Whatever the case, Graham seemed to be one of those 'before you call, I answer' people.

"You must be starving," he said. This was followed by some of the most glorious words I have ever heard. "We can stop on the way back at McDonald's. There's one on the way."

For the next 45 minutes or so, I got to know the two men who were looking after me. Graham had been in the British Army and was now pursuing a career as a paramedic. His explanation of what I was about to go through in theatre was so clear and concise that I ended up telling him he was a born educator. "You should be standing in front of your peers showing them how to communicate," I said. Dave, the driver, had been in the corporate world, become fed up with it all, joined the ambulance service, but was now starting the process of becoming a full-time fireman. He was starting at an age when many of his peers would be preparing to retire from the fire service.

Graham had now rigged me up to a monitor and was checking my readings when he asked a question.

"We often only get to see patients while they're in the ambulance, driving to an operation, then driving them back. As part of our training, we are allowed to go into theatre and observe what you go through there as well. Would you mind if we do that?"

I thought for a moment. Having two paramedics in theatre in addition to all the people who would already be assigned to my care was a big bonus. It would improve the odds of me being safe in the event of an emergency. I therefore said yes.

"Thank you," Dave said from the front. "To be honest," he continued, "it gets a bit boring when it's just a matter of transporting patients to and from hospital. We want to be with you in the middle part of your journey as well. It's more interesting."

I don't think Dave had any inkling how interesting it was going to be for him personally.

Minutes later, we arrived at the ward in Margate Hospital. By now, I was desperate for a pee. This was a familiar part of my morning routine in hospital, and a direct consequence of the diuretic injection Abi had given me at dawn. I was getting used to having to use the toilet on a regular basis in the hours leading up to lunch. Today was no exception, so I asked the nurse on duty – an obviously gifted team leader called Naomi – if I could use the facilities. She said yes and I was given one of those rather fetching 'portable male urinals.' It would not be the last one I used as I waited for my 9.00am procedure.

Graham and Dave bade me a fond farewell, saying they would pick me up after the operation, and I was left lying on a bed in the ward. I will describe the actual procedure that followed in more detail in the next chapter, but for now I want to keep the spotlight trained on Graham and Dave, especially Dave, because what happened next was so unexpected it's still hard to believe it happened.

The operation that followed was performed under local anaesthetic. This means that I was conscious of everything that was going on around me.

A short time into the three-hour procedure, I heard a loud crashing sound coming from somewhere behind me.

At this point, the surgeon stopped what he was doing, as did everyone else. All heads turned towards an area of theatre where there was a kind of cordoned-off section – a makeshift viewing station. It was there, behind a windowed partition (as I recall) that my two companions in green were observing what the surgeon was doing to me. They had the advantage of closeup images on a monitor next to them.

And that was the problem.

Seeing the knife do its work, Dave fainted.

And he fell.

Dave smashed his chin on the corner of a table. Blood went everywhere and the place looked like a crime scene. Hence the almighty clattering and the commotion that followed.

Yes, you did just read that.

A paramedic fainted!

Dave was escorted to A&E in the hospital.

He needed three stitches.

I have never heard of this happening before. Afterwards, Graham came to apologise.

"I'm so sorry. We won't be able to drive you back to the William Harvey. Dave has had to head back to base. You've been assigned new drivers for your return."

Before he left, I had to ask a question.

"Why did Dave pass out, do you think?"

It had to be asked. Paramedics are not supposed to do this. Dave, it turns out, was squeamish.

"I can't say for sure, but I think it has something to do with the context of the operating theatre. Dave's used to seeing things outside that context and after the event. He just couldn't deal with watching it live and in that environment."

I nodded as I lay on the bed.

"I'm sorry we never got to have that McDonald's," Graham said. He seemed genuinely disappointed.

"That's alright. Just give Dave my love."

Graham needn't have worried. The all-seeing eyes of Naomi the nurse had already sensed I was hungry. She knew that I had been NBM since 6.00pm the previous day. She turned up with sandwiches after Graham had left. They might not have been one of Ronald's meal deals, but to me they tasted amazing.

After I had eaten – and peed several more times – the new drivers appeared. They were kind and friendly too. As they began the journey back to Ashford, I couldn't help thinking of Dave, the queasy paramedic. Sometimes, we forget that paramedics and nurses are just ordinary, regular people like us. There's not some huge line in the sand with patients on one side and medics on the other. We're all on the same side of the line. We all have vulnerabilities.

It's like back in the days when I used to be a vicar. Parishioners would look at me as something or someone different – six days invisible, one day incomprehensible as the saying goes. "What's clerical thrombosis?" I was once asked. I said I didn't know. "A clot in the pulpit", the guy replied. At times, people were less cynical and more idealistic. I am convinced that some regarded me as an otherworldly being, hermetically sealed from the muckiness of mortal life. I remember in one sermon saying that I even believed that some people I knew didn't think I ever peed. If only they could see me now. Thanks to my regular dose of diuretics, I was peeing for England.

People like Dave and Graham are just like you and me, which is why they deserve our respect. They are, in many ways, much more commendable because they have committed their lives to caring for others. But they are still human.

I thought of Dave returning to base and all his colleagues seeing his wound. Well, it's not easy to hide something that visible, is it? I shook my head. Poor chap. How was he ever going to live that down? Perhaps it was a good thing he was going to join the fire service. But then my mind started working in overdrive. Surely, he would see some horrible sights as a fireman too.

I offered up a little prayer under my breath.

I say prayer.

But it was more exclamation than intercession.

"God help him!"

CHAPTER 14

SAILING THE CARDIAC SEA

"The doctor will be here soon," Naomi, the nurse in charge, said. "He comes to work on his bike." She looked at me and added, "I should warn you. He's a fan of heavy metal music. He'll have it on in the background during the procedure."

"What's his name?" I asked.

"Dr Ward," she replied.

I couldn't help smiling. My doctor the day before had been called Vaney. This one was called Ward. Maybe tomorrow I'd be examined by someone called Catheter. I began to feel as if I had been transported into the hospital set of a *Carry-On* film.

As the clock pushed towards 9.00am, the great man entered. He spoke to Naomi and then approached my bed.

"We'll wheel you in in a minute," he said.

Naomi had already asked me to sign a consent form. She had also brought me a gown to put on. You know the type. A flimsy single-piece, shin-length garment that ties up at the back. I say 'ties up'; that implies the process is straightforward. It isn't, as I'm sure you know if you've ever had to wear one. They tend not to fit that well and tying bows – or any other kind of knots for that matter – is no easy task when you're doing it behind your own back. I managed to get some kind of knot done, but I felt very naked – which I was – and the gown appeared to me to be only barely attached to my body – which it was. I was allowed to keep on my underpants because there was no metal in them.

Having finished pleasantries with Dr Ward, I was pushed through some double doors into the theatre. After being transferred to a narrow bed, I decided to lie back and relax. I could see about five or six people milling around me, getting themselves ready for the procedure. There seemed to be a second-in-command, as it were. He was not the talkative type. He had a somewhat moody demeanour and seemed to me to want to get on with things. All he said was, "Make sure you lie still." Others were more personable, asking me if I was okay, making small talk as they attached me to an ECG monitor that measured blood pressure, oxygen levels in my blood, heart rate, and so on.

"Do you want a sedative?" Dr Ward asked.

"Oh yes," I replied.

The good doctor asked one of his colleagues to do the honours and a few minutes later I was gazing at the X-Ray machine above my head as if it was something out of *Close Encounters of the Third Kind*. By the time the drug had taken effect, I was in the most euphoric state I have ever experienced. I have never felt anything like it. I was floating in a liquid state of unimaginable tranquillity. The whole experience was positively oceanic.

Other drugs were injected too, including antibiotics and pain relief before the now very good doctor – in my bleary eyes at least – covered the left side of my face with a surgical drape to protect me from seeing what he was doing and from having my vision marred by what CSI detectives call 'blood spatter.' Having half my face veiled was not an unpleasant thing at all. It just added to the now overwhelming sense of sleepy reverie. Bizarre as it sounds, I felt enveloped. Dr Ward had put me at my ease, and whatever it was he had used as a sedative had made me feel at one with everyone and everything around me – even Mister Grumpy in the sky-blue surgical cap.

The good and quite wonderful doctor now shaved my upper body and used an antiseptic solution to clean the left side of my chest just beneath the collarbone. This was where he was going to insert my pacemaker. We should pause here and talk about this extremely expensive and sophisticated gadget. This little marvel is called a Cardiac Resynchronization Therapy Defibrillator – CRTD for short - and is a small, metal, battery-powered device. The battery life on mine is about 7 years, so I won't need a replacement for a long time. If I had not had heart failure, my heart rate would have been controlled by my own natural pacemaker. However, I had an irregular heart-signalling condition known as a 'bifascicular block'. I therefore needed help to send electrical signals to the two lower chambers of my heart. That's where the CRTD came in, which is a biventricular pacemaker. This does two main jobs. First, it resynchronizes the two lower chambers of my heart so that they are working together properly. Secondly, it corrects dangerous heart rhythms. This is why the **D** in CRT**D** is important. D stands for defibrillator. The CRTD achieves these miraculous results through tiny leads inserted into the heart. These carry electrical impulses. It's quite some gadget.

The beatific doctor, having now shaved and swabbed the area, inserted a local anaesthetic all around the place where he was about to make an incision. I was aware of a slight stinging sensation as the needle punctured my skin, but that soon left and was replaced by a numbness that formed the perfect accompaniment to my mood-altered state. All this was rendered even more surreal by the heavy-metal songs coming from what sounded like a radio somewhere to my left. I half expected Judas Priest to blast out Painkiller, but I can't honestly say I was conscious of anything more than a distant noise, and a happy humming from someone near to me.

Once I was, to quote Pink Floyd, 'comfortably numb', the celestial doctor set to work. He made a cut just under my left collarbone. I felt nothing. The anaesthetic was doing its job just fine. His hands then started to move with the precision and excellence of an artist who has performed this task a thousand times, even though it's both complex and challenging. He inserted IV lines into a vein that leads to my heart. He then fed two wires into that vein and into parts of my heart. I was aware of all this happening because he calmly talked me through what he was doing. He kept track of his and my progress by looking at the images on a large monitor to my right.

Having tested the first two leads using an electric impulse, he set about inserting a third and final lead. He explained that the first two were straightforward, but this third had to be fed down a vein that was trickier to navigate. It would take longer, he said, and he would need to take care not to touch the sides of the vein as he charted a course around the bends along the way. When he had managed to get to the right part of the heart, he would need to make sure the end of the lead was properly attached to the muscle, a feat that sounded to me like dragging an anchor until it dug into the seabed.

After what seemed no time at all – because of my altered state of consciousness – but was in all probability a long time, the genius on my left told me he had managed to secure the third lead. Somewhere deep within the recesses of my tranquilised mind I saw him as an ancient seafarer making his way across the great ocean of my heart. In a moment of silence in the theatre, I could not help myself. I declared, "You are the Christopher Columbus of the Cardiac Sea." No sooner were the words out of my mouth than a tiny part of my neo-cortex questioned both my rationality and sense of etiquette. But the perfect doctor didn't seem to mind at all, so the euphoria displaced any trace of concern. I closed my eyes and set sail with him.

From this moment on, Dr Ward attached the leads to the pacemaker and conducted some tests before inserting the CRTD in the pocket he had made earlier in my chest. At some stage during this last phase, he asked me what I did for a living. I replied that I was a writer, mainly of novels. I added, "Although the thing I most enjoy is reviewing Lego products for a men's magazine." In retrospect, I'm not even sure that's true. I enjoy all the writing I do, including this. But it seemed like the right thing to say at the time.

"I love Lego too," Dr Ward said.

"No!" I said, possibly overreacting slightly under the

influence of whatever was intensifying my emotions. In fact, they were so heightened that I could have quite easily broken into the Lego movie song, "Everything is awesome," but instead, I calmed myself down and engaged in a sensible conversation.

"What was the last thing you built?"

"The Castle of the Heron," he replied. "We went on holiday to Japan, and we visited the actual place. I decided when we returned that I'd buy the Lego version."

I'll be honest here. I knew the set the doctor was describing. I had seen it reviewed on YouTube. It's a beautiful build, but it's not my thing. I didn't say that. I told him that my last build had been the house from the Pixar movie called *Up*. Cherith and I had visited the actual house on which the animated house is modelled. It's in Utah where my twin sister lives. I loved the film, and I loved the Lego.

The conversation from there progressed to more highbrow topics – the state of the NHS, how things used to be for him in times past, and how his attitude towards his profession and the institution had changed over the years. All the while, I was thinking about him building his Japanese castle, imagining how relaxing and therapeutic that must be if you do a job like his at a time like this.

And then I had a thought. When I came home, I would ask Cherith to buy me the Castle of the Heron. Not the real one in Japan. The Lego build. I'd put it together when I was well enough to do some Lego again. I'd then put the finished product somewhere in our home and, every time I saw it, I would say a silent thank you in my resynchronized heart for the man who was standing next to me.

And I had every reason to be deeply thankful. The

person who just happened to be available for me that Friday morning was one of the UK's top cardiologists and a man who specialises in pacemakers. What I did not know until later is that Dr Kevin Ward is an esteemed expert in device therapy, specifically the kind of therapy that treats life-threatening cardiac arrhythmias and heart failure. It was one of these devices that he had implanted in my body with such skill that day, and it was precisely these medical issues that this device was designed to treat. Dr Ward is in fact so well respected among his fellow medics that in 2008 he was invited by his cardiology peers to become a fellow of the Royal College of Physicians.

In the last minutes we spent together, Dr Ward pressed down on the CRTD in my chest, pushing it into the pocket, making sure it was secured in place through some impressive thumps with his fist. This momentary impression of Mike Tyson was the only time in the three hours when I felt any discomfort, but he had taken the time and trouble to explain why he had to do this, so I took the short-term pain for the sake of the long-term gain – a heart that stood a great chance of pumping efficiently, and a life I could enjoy again.

Dr Ward finished by closing the opening in my chest using dissolvable stitches and placing a dressing over the wound site. I now had a device in my chest that was delivering electrical impulses to my heart, harmonizing the two chambers that had been out of sync for a long time. These two leads were stimulating the two chambers to pump at the same time. A third would send impulses to the muscles of my heart whenever it was beating too quickly – something that could cause fatal or life-threatening heart rhythms. These are known as VT and VF - ventricular tachycardia and ventricular fibrillation. The defib would provide shock treatment and save my life.

My little grandson would later become rather enamoured with this device. "Grandpa has a robot heart," he would say to his friends. In a sense, he's right. Thanks to Dr Ward, I have a state-of-the-art device that gives me a great chance not only of living better but living longer. Dr Vaney had described it as a *turbo* pacemaker the previous evening. I liked the word turbo. It reminded me of Arnold Schwarzenegger in the film *Jingle All the Way* – something I loved watching with my kids every Christmas. As a father, Arnie's desperation to get his son the perfect Christmas present was something that chimed with my own experience. Arnie had become Turbo Man in his efforts to secure the gift. Thanks to Dr Ward, I was now Turbo Man.

But how effective would this turbo be? Would my robot heart allow me to sleep again? Would it bring an end to my persistent coughing? Would it drive away the fatigue and restore my energy? Take away my urinary problems? Eradicate the dizziness? Stabilize my blood pressure? Would it do what others said it would do?

Maybe it was the aftereffects of the sedative, but as I left Margate and returned with two new ambulance drivers to Ashford, I sensed a deep assurance that the answer was yes to all and my mood became as bright and cloudless as the Kent sky.

DAY 6
SATURDAY

MAY 18TH 2024

And there was evening, and there was morning - the sixth day.

Genesis 1:31

CHAPTER 15

A VERY IMPORTANT PERSON

At the start of World War 2, my adoptive father – Philip Stibbe – volunteered for military service and joined the Royal Sussex Regiment. He became part of General Wingate's Army and fought behind enemy lines in India. One day, he was severely wounded while fighting in a battle in the jungle. A bullet passed through the front of his chest and out of his back. It missed his heart by a centimetre.

The rule during this covert operation was that the wounded would have to be left behind so as not to slow down the army. A Gurkha rifleman nicknamed Moto said he would stay with Dad and look after him. He would dress his wounds and forage for food and water in the local villages. This he did until Dad's strength began to increase, and his health take a turn for the better.

One day, however, Moto did not return.

As the hours wore on, Dad became more and more anxious for Moto's safety. In the end, he managed to get to his feet, use a makeshift crutch, and shuffle along to a nearby village. There was a clearing in the centre of the huts. Underneath the shade of a tree, several enemy soldiers were sheltering, their rifles next to them. When Dad saw them, all he could think of was Moto's welfare. As the soldiers gathered their weapons and started to run towards him, Dad shouted, "Moto! Moto! They've found me! Stay away!"

But Moto, Dad was later to discover, could not hear him. Those soldiers had heard that there was a British officer hiding somewhere in the jungle. They were desperate to capture him. They had found Moto, interrogated him, and tortured him. In the end, when Moto would not divulge my father's whereabouts, the soldiers shot him in the head, killing him instantly.

My father always regarded Moto as a hero, and he was unable until the very end of his life to put into words the debt of gratitude he owed to this remarkable, courageous Nepalese warrior. Dad would spend most of the rest of the war as a prisoner in Rangoon jail, a place of unimaginable torment and degradation. After the war, he would give himself to the service of young people as a teacher and ultimately a headteacher at Norwich School. Right to the end, he made it his aim to live a life worthy of the sacrifice Moto had made. He never stopped remembering the love the rifleman had shown.

Why am I telling you this?

Firstly, because over the last 100 years or so we have become in the UK a country that's obsessed with celebrities. Whether we idealise or demonise them, we can't get enough of them. Their air-brushed faces are on our screens all the time. People seem fixated on what these characters are saying and doing.

How many of them merit such idolising and adulating attention? What do they really add to our lives? Are they worth the money they amass or the airtime they receive? Do they deserve to be celebrated? Have they done anything that is so noble, selfless, humble, creative, and positive that they deserve the kind of attention we seem so eager to give them? Do they possess a character of such integrity and authenticity that the glare can be said to be justified?

I had already been asking questions like this before March 2020 when the Covid-19 pandemic brought the UK and the world to a screeching halt. But when this event was in full swing, the questions became even more acute as celebrities started using social media to broadcast their thoughts from the safety and luxury of their mansions. Can anyone remember anything any of them said or did? The only person I can remember is Ricky Gervais who used his savage humour to criticise celebrities for thinking they had any right to moralise given their immense privilege. Ricky did this while ironically being a celebrity himself and ironically lecturing the lecturers! The paradox was not lost on him either. It was part of the 'joke'.

Meanwhile, the then prime minister – himself a celebrity from the world of entertainment, and certainly not a hero - decided it would be a good idea if everyone in the UK clapped the tireless NHS workers who were expending themselves by treating the sick and saving lives. He encouraged us to stand outside our front doors and applaud them at an agreed time one evening in the week. Even he seemed to understand that it wasn't the celebrities who were worthy of our praise during the pandemic. He had caught the Covid virus himself. His life had been saved by NHS staff. Somewhere under that mop of a hairdo, his brain had a moment of clarity about who are the true heroes in the UK. And it's not people like him.

It's abundantly clear to me that this man wanted to go down in history as a contemporary Winston Churchill. While we were not at war, he did see the virus as his battlefront. It goes without saying that the man in question did not achieve his ambition. All he was, and all he'll ever be, is a celebrity – a man who learned to play the part of a clown at Eton College, and then carried on performing the role on TV, and finally in no 10 Downing Street. Meanwhile, the country he led was rescued not by him nor by his government but by ordinary people in blue uniforms and white coats who gave themselves for a cause greater than themselves every day and night for the duration of the pandemic. These honest, humble souls are the true heroes. Many NHS staff lost their lives. Some who had Covid still had to go to work. Others are now suffering the long-term and severe effects of the virus without proper recognition or support.

Maybe by now you're beginning to hear my recovering heart. I have very little time for celebrities, except those like the late, great Paul O'Grady who use their platform to change the world – in Paul's case, for dogs. I only have a limited amount of respect cells in my brain these days, and these are directed not towards celebrities but heroes. Heroes are ordinary, faceless people who give themselves for a cause that transcends their self-interest. Their focus is on improving the lives of other people – or, if not people, then dogs, polar bears, whales, trees, oceans, icecaps, and so on. These are the real heroes. You may never see their names in lights. You may never read their names in the honours' lists.

You may never hear them interviewed on Desert Island Discs or the Graham Norton Show. But they are all around us every day. One spends their life fostering children. Another goes to a school for children with special educational needs and enriches the lives of the kids they teach. Another, a volunteer, dons their RNLI regulation kit and heads out to save those in peril on the sea. I could go on and on. These people are heroes, not celebrities. A troll has a hard heart, and a bot has no heart, but even trolls and bots can't dis a hero.

While I was in hospital, I met so many ordinary people I would regard as heroes. I'm thinking right now of the nurse who was on duty at the crack of my first dawn in the William Harvey Hospital, who put Cherith at ease when she phoned to find out how I was, and who escorted me with such care and good humour from the Triage area to the first proper ward where I stayed.

I'm thinking of the nurses in the Rapid Assessment Ward who spent so much time all day and evening attending to a man lying on a bed just outside my bay – a man who had come in either high or inebriated (or both) and who had them running around after him for about twelve hours, even demanding different sandwiches to the ones he had requested. In the end, he decided to discharge himself without permission. When he had gone, the resilient nurses brushed themselves down and got on with helping other patients.

I'm thinking of the women who wheeled the trolly into Saint Bartholmew and supplied me with cups of tea and sandwiches at mealtimes every day and night.

All these good souls are heroes in my eyes.

One stands out in my memory, a tall young man called Vippin. He looked after me in Saint Bartholmew and he did so with a deep and sincere compassion. He worked shifts that lasted over twelve hours, several of which were nights. He woke me up shortly before he was due to go home on Saturday morning. I'm talking somewhere around 5.30am-6.00am. By that time, I fully trusted him as he administered several daily injections through my cannula, and one in my tummy. To this mix of medicines was added some painkillers. The wound site from the implantation of my CRTD the previous day was very bruised. Vippin made sure I was given the right pain relief meds, counting the hours between giving them with meticulous care.

That morning, I could tell Vippin was exhausted. His eyes were not as bright and joyful as usual, and his face was pale from the night he had spent on duty. I wanted to encourage him, so I devised a plan. Next to me on the wall was a whiteboard. On it, the nurse on duty who was responsible for my care had to write their name. When their shift ended and a new nurse took over, they would erase the previous name and write theirs. That morning, Vippin's name was still on the whiteboard, so I asked him to bring me a non-permanent pen and a rag. He asked me why, but I told him to trust me.

When he came back, I rubbed out what he had written nearly twelve hours before and I started writing. The first line was in capital letters, CROWN PRINCE VIPPIN. The second read, V.I.P. Very Important Person.

"Thank you for looking after me so well," I said. "You really are a remarkable person."

Vippin's eyes filled.

"I want to take a photo of this," he whispered.

Vippin produced his mobile phone, took a photo, and sent it straight to his wife.

"Your father must be very proud of you," I said, my voice soft and low so as not to wake the other men.

"He's back home in India, very sick," he answered.

He then told me about what his dad was going through, and what he was doing to help, even while being a dad himself, and a medic working long hours in the hospital. I told him he was doing a great job and that I thought he was a remarkable man.

Affirmation is a powerful thing, especially when people are worn out and deflated. As he read the whiteboard again, Vippin's eyes regained their lustre and his face its colour.

I could tell he was very touched by this conversation – the last we would have before I left the following day (Sunday). When he gave me my blood-thinning injection, the needle stung a little more than usual and he must have seen the faintest wince. He apologised so profusely I thought he was going to burst into tears. When he left to continue his rounds, he hugged me, then turned to the whiteboard one more time and gazed at my version of the honour's list.

What do all these heroes have in common? I remember Stephen Fry saying something at Norwich School where my father was headteacher. Stephen was asked to come and give a speech at the big annual prize-giving ceremony. He told the young people and parents that he had been all over the world and met many very famous and wealthy people. But, he added, he didn't remember those that were well-known and rich. He only remembered those who were kind. Kindness is the common denominator in all the heroes I met at the hospitals I attended during my time receiving medical care. They were kind to me, and they were kind to Cherith.

As that Saturday wore on, I was the recipient of many more acts of kindness. It was during one of these that I was overwhelmed by another example of providence. Early in the afternoon, I was being wheeled in bed to another part of the hospital. I was struck by the looks I was getting from people bearing flowers who were clearly on their way to visit their loved ones. We British are capable of being bawdy and boisterous at times, sometimes belligerent and badly behaved. But at the core of our being, we are also compassionate people – people whose hearts beat with empathy as quickly as our eyes fill with tears. Just watch Gogglebox on Channel 4 whenever it's Stand up to Cancer night. We British do care about each other. Deep down. I saw it in the concerned looks and kind smiles of those I passed on the way.

Perhaps the kindest of all was the lad steering my bed through the hospital and doing so with such skill he never once touched the walls of the corridors or the frames of the doors. He was a man who loved his cat. He showed me a photo of it. To be honest, the kitty was a little overweight, but this was not the porter's doing. "My mother," he said. "She lives with me. But she doesn't do what she's told. She gives my cat too much food. Extra meals. So now he's a fat cat."

I offered him my solution. "Maybe you should use the same tactics with your mother. Use food. Stop feeding your mother until she stops overfeeding the cat."

He told me this was a great idea.

When the laughter died down, I asked him if he was from the Nepalese community nearby. Most of Britain's Nepalis live in the southeast of England with Kent – the Garden of England - their address. The Gurkha Rifles are stationed in Folkestone, very near where I live. There are restaurants and shops with the names Everest and Gurkha. If you've never eaten Nepalese cuisine, you've missed something extraordinary. Cherith adores *Momos*.

Anyway, it turned out that my cat-loving porter was indeed from this community. As he told me that, I thought back to the previous November. I had held a Remembrance Service at our local pub – the same pub I mentioned earlier, the one frequented by Spitfire pilots during the Battle of Britain. I had invited some leading figures from the local Nepalese community to come and celebrate with us. I had wanted to give thanks to God for the Gurkha rifleman. When they came, I presented them with a copy of my father's war memoir, *Return Via Rangoon*, and we gave thanks as a congregation for Moto's life and sacrifice. It was a very moving event; there were some tearful eyes around the bar that Sunday evening.

Now, in the William Harvey Hospital in Ashford, on a Saturday afternoon in May 2024, I was struck by another example of synchronicity. Here I was being helped by a young British man of Nepalese ancestry just as my father had been over eighty years ago. I too was wounded in the chest, though by a scalpel and a fist, not by the bullet from an enemy rifle. I too was being tended and carried by a person whose people originally hailed from Nepal.

I remembered how Moto looked after Dad with such kindness and heroism. And for a synchronised heartbeat or two, I was overwhelmed by a sense of history repeating itself.

CHAPTER 16

SHE'S ONE IN A MILLION

The mission given to my cat-loving porter was to get me to the X-Ray department. There is a very slight danger when a pacemaker is fitter that the left lung can be damaged, so an X-Ray was requested to make sure it was still in good shape. For that reason, I had another companion beside the porter – a young nurse whose job was to escort me into the X-Ray ward. She was there to monitor my condition and call for help if I needed it. When we arrived, there was a short wait before I could be wheeled in for the X-Ray. We got into a conversation.

"Who's that nice woman who visits you in the ward? Is she your partner?" she asked.

"She's my wife," I replied.

"She's been with you all the time."

"I know. I'm very lucky."

Cherith had been with me every day until bedtime. She has told me since I've come home that she would have slept in the chair next to my bed had I not kicked her out each night at 9pm. 9pm has, for a long time, been the hour when I start thinking of sleep. Two close friends, Saul and Rachel (about whom, more later), refer to it affectionately as 'milky-drink time' in honour of an overnight visit they made when I offered them an Ovaltine to take upstairs with them when they were far from ready for bed. I disappeared upstairs, leaving them twiddling their thumbs. Cherith, in honour of this quirk, agreed each night – reluctantly I might add – to drive home at 9.00pm.

The nurse smiled.

"We've all been commenting on her," she said. After a pause, there was the softest and faintest sigh as she added, "I hope I have someone like that one day."

This was not the moment for making jokes about my wife. I could tell the nurse really meant it and my heart went out to her. Mother Teresa once said that the greatest disease in the world is not tuberculosis or malaria; it's loneliness. People are dying for a lack of companionship, a lack of love. This is true not just of those who live on their own, but those who live with someone who is emotionally distant, who does not engage with them at a heart-to-heart level. Someone once said that loneliness is not the state of being physically on your own; it's not having anyone to share your heart with, someone who is happy to share their heart with you. Everyone needs a Cherith – someone who's not just committed to being with you physically but being there emotionally. Right at that moment I wished with all my recovering heart for this nurse to have her dream come true, and the wish that I nurtured transformed itself into a simple, silent prayer. May she find her soulmate too, wherever and whoever they are.

People like Cherith are one in a million. I know you think I'm speaking figuratively, but I'm not. Cherith and I got married in June 2015 at Wellington House, Canterbury. That was a registry office wedding. We decided to have a wedding blessing and full reception at Christmas time later that year. We chose the stunning location of Wiston House in West Sussex, which has a fine old chapel adjacent to the main building. My late mother had left me enough money to pay for the whole event. Wanting to have a celebration that Cherith would never forget, she and I planned for our happy day with sky-high expectations. When it duly arrived, we were not disappointed. The grounds were powdered with snow and the drawing room – a roaring log fire in the grate – was adorned with a tall Christmas tree and decorations. It was the most perfect day, a dream come true.

Only one task remained unprepared. Distracted by all the practical preparations, I realised as I woke up that morning that I had not written a short talk for my slot after the reception or afternoon dinner. I remember lying in bed as dawn broke on the great day and thinking, what do I want to say about the love of my life? How would I sum up this most beautiful of women? Straightaway, a thought struck me like a match - a brief encapsulation of her qualities. *Cherith is the prettiest, grittiest, and wittiest of them all.* I would speak from the heart about all three of these luminous virtues.

I won't bore you with the details of each of the three superlatives, but I will just say something about the word 'prettiest', not because I'm superficial and only appreciate her external beauty, but because it is relevant to the point I want to make in this chapter. When I say Cherith is one in a million, I mean it literally. She outshines every other woman I have ever met or will ever meet when it comes to natural, unvarnished beauty. She is truly one of a kind.

Google is a great get-out-of-jail-free card in situations like these, so I entered a topic in its search engine. Ever since I first met Cherith, two of the things that have stood out for me are her long red hair and her deep blue eyes. The two make for a most striking combination. They dazzle me every day. And I mean that too. So, off I went looking at articles about red hair and blue eyes. To cut a very long story short, I discovered that it is a known scientific fact that this alluring fusion of features is very rare indeed. Statistically, it is at least one in a million. The odds of having both red hair and blue eyes are about 0.17%. It is the rarest colour combination in human beings. 90% of the world's population is dark-haired. Blonde comes in second. But only 1-2% have red hair, and fewer still have red hair and blue eyes. When I say that Cherith is the prettiest, she really is just that. She is as rare as a red wolf.

Why am I telling you this? It is simply because I am in awe of Cherith's devotion. There were strict visiting hours on all the wards in the William Harvey Hospital. Cherith told me she would respect the wishes of the medics, but if they did not ask her to leave, she would take that as permission to stay. So, every day and evening, stay she did. She was awake every morning when I sent her a text. I am talking very early some days – 5.00am. That is so unlike her. Cherith loves a lie-in and baulks at having to drag herself out of bed. But here she was, alert to every piece of information I sent, asking what I needed, bringing a coffee with her when she walked into the ward every morning after I had been given my daily dose of requested porridge. She would sit by my bed all day and evening in St Bartholomew. When I needed a nap, she would head over to Terry, who was lying in a bed opposite me, and chat with him. She also chatted with Joe who was recovering in the bay next to Terry, found out he needed a razor and gel, and bought both for him, refusing to take any payment.

On this same day, something happened that I think says everything about her. If you were to ask Cherith if she shed any tears at any point while she was with me on the wards that week, she would answer, "Yes. Once. On Saturday morning." For the rest of the time, her tears were reserved for one conversation with her mother. She did not want to add to my burdens the sight of her in emotional pain. But on that day, all her levees were destroyed by a tsunami of tears – not tears of agony, but ones of ecstasy. For months she had watched me wrestling with a cough that sounded dreadful. She had witnessed firsthand the effects of that cough on my sleep, or lack of it. She had listened with deep concern to my nocturnal tossing and turning in the beanbag on the floor of our bedroom. Now, 24 hours after my CRTD had been inserted in my chest, everything was beginning to look a whole lot sunnier. "When I entered the ward that Saturday morning," she would later tell me, "I saw you lying on your back, fast asleep. I couldn't believe the difference in you. I was so grateful, I just burst into tears."

Whenever I bring myself to tell the story of my seven days of cardiac care, I of course express my gratitude for all the medics who cared for me, especially the doctor who told me to go to hospital (Dr Edward), the doctor who made sure I was diagnosed correctly and bumped me to the top of the operating list (Dr Anne Louise), and the doctor who performed the operation with the manual dexterity of a Picasso (Dr Kevin). I will forever be grateful to them. But most of all, I'm grateful for Cherith. I really couldn't have got through these seven days without the prettiest, wittiest, and grittiest of them all. And by 'them all', I don't mean a long list of girlfriends. I'm not that kind of guy. I mean human beings in general. I regard myself as undeserving of this devotion. I have never known anything like it. Nor had the nurse who commented about it outside the X-Ray department.

Cherith would want me to say that she might not have been there at all if it hadn't been for Julia, her line manager at work. With the blessing of Luke, her acting head, Cherith was given compassionate leave for two weeks. Without their kindness, and the support of her friends at work – especially Mel and Laura – Cherith would not have been able to support me in the way she did. Along with Rachel, her best friend back in Northern Ireland, these brilliant people stepped up when she needed them most. She was very thankful for their support.

With their help, Cherith spent all week doing what she does so well – being one in a million. She kept in touch with our family and friends, giving them daily updates. She asked those whom she knew to be spiritual to pray for my full recovery, which they did faithfully and, I'm sure, to great effect. She brought me grapes and orange juice. She sat by my side and did crosswords with me. And when she returned home late every night, she did everything she could to make the place ready for my return, including buying a patient's pillow, a portable table for my meals, and new bedsheets. No one could have done more. Everything I said about her at our wedding reception was true.

Prettiest, yes.

Grittiest, yes.

Wittiest, yes.

When I came home, and when I was strong enough, she decided we hadn't had a holiday in a long time and that I needed one if I was to recover. She found somewhere near where I was brought up in North Norfolk, near the sea, because she knew and knows how therapeutic I find being near the ocean. Since it was last minute, we rented somewhere affordable and cosy, and off we went with the dogs to spend long hours on the expansive and uncrowded sands of Holkham Beach – a place where I enjoyed many days as a boy.

On one of these sunny days, I watched her walking along the path towards the beach, one I had trod countless times as a child. I was suddenly overwhelmed by how beautiful she is, and how seeing her walking among the pine trees on our way to the sea was the nearest thing to heaven I had ever experienced. In that moment, a poem was born – a sonnet which I later wrote for her as a little token of my appreciation for all she had done for me in hospital. I didn't think it was possible to love her any more than I already did, but at that moment, I fell even more in love with her. Later, as Wordsworth once put it, my emotion was recollected in tranquillity. Remembering my spontaneous overflow of powerful feelings, I recaptured the moment in poetic form. I know some of you may take issue with the number of beats in each line (four rather than the normal five in this kind of poetic form) but let me just say I wanted to do something different and unusual to match the uniqueness of my subject, so that's intentional.

She walks among the ageless pines
Her bare feet in the needled sand:
Her freckled face the sun outshines,
As through this seaside Neverland
She heads along the boarded way
Towards the distant grassy dunes
Where ring-necked plovers strut and play
And sanderlings sing croaky tunes.
When I was young my soft-skinned feet
Would race across this endless beach.
I never thought I'd one day meet
A girl whose beauty would outreach
The splendour of this sand, this sea, this sky
I love so much. How wrong was I.

Four months after leaving hospital, it was Cherith's turn

to be looked after by me. To cut a long story short, she started showing some worrying symptoms. A visit to the doctor followed, and some tests, and then came the day when the clouds gathered overhead. Cherith phoned me from the school where she works. She sounded worried, close to tears. It was obvious something was terribly wrong.

Cherith is made of true grit. It takes a lot to rattle her.

"The doctor has just phoned," she said. "He's put me on the NHS's two-week pathway for people who need immediate assessment. He said twice in his call that he was concerned, that it might be cancer, but that I was to try not to worry."

It's hard to put into words how we both felt at this unexpected reversal. After months of Cherith looking after me, it was time now for me to look after her. Yes, she is a strong independent woman, but we all need a shoulder and a hug when we receive news like this. We all need support when our health is under threat.

And so, I began two weeks of carrying my beloved wife in the same year she had carried me. We treated every day together as a gift. Every walk with the dogs was like gold dust slipping through our fingers – bright, gleaming, fleeting, transient, but infinitely precious. Every time we held hands, our palms pressed more closely to each other than ever before, relishing the touch.

When the time you have left together is less than you thought, every second is a priceless gift.

I remember when I was 15 having a conversation with a lovely man called Tim Potts. Our family and his were friends. I was sitting with him outside the back of his house, overlooking a vibrant garden. We were drinking something cold and delicious.

"What do you think the secret of life is?" he asked.

I said, "To live every day as if it's your last but without ever getting morbid or morose about it."

I remember being as surprised as he was by what I had just said. I had been thinking deeply about life, yes, but I hadn't formulated my personal philosophy in such a terse way before, so I was more than a little startled by my own words.

"There's a lot of wisdom in that," Tim said.

I forget how the conversation went afterwards, but I have never forgotten my reply, and I have tried to live in the light of what Tim called that 'wisdom' ever since, never more so than when Cherith and I found ourselves walking in trepidation through the valley of the shadow. In the end, it proved to be a false alarm and something treatable with a course of antibiotics. But until we knew that outcome, we lived with an attitude that changed both of us. The things that seemed important before – issues to do with jobs and money, for example – became very unimportant indeed. What mattered was shrugging off everything that's trivial and revelling in what's essential.

Many years ago, when we were just getting to know each other, Cherith looked at me and said, "I've got your back."

She's always had my back.

And I have always had hers.

If you don't already, I really hope you find someone who has yours. Just as I hope and pray that the nurse who wheeled me to the X-Ray department finds someone who has hers.

DAY 7
SUNDAY

MAY 19TH 2024

By the seventh day God had finished the work he had been doing; so, on the seventh day he rested from all his work.

Genesis 2:2

CHAPTER 17

RETURNING WITH THE ELIXIR

I describe myself as a kind of narrative paramedic. When I'm not writing books, I'm helping other storytellers to fix the problems with their stories. As I've developed this over the last decade, there have been several go-to resources. One of these is a twelve-step plot structure for storytellers called 'The Hero's Journey.' Based on Joseph Campbell's extensive work on myths, the hero's journey centres on a lead character, often someone quite ordinary, who gives themselves in a cause greater than themselves. This task, quest, or mission is a journey involving three main stages. In Act 1, the hero is in their ordinary world. In Act 2, they enter a special world which stretches them to their limits. In Act 3, they return to their ordinary world having been transformed by their experiences. They bring with them treasure of some kind that they've found along the way.

In his influential book *The Writer's Journey,* Christopher Vogler, a former Disney consultant, showed how the twelve steps of the hero's journey fit into this three-act structure. I have used these 12 steps frequently in my coaching and teaching, especially in one-to-one sessions as well as group seminars with fiction writers. I have always stressed that this 12-step journey is a guide not a straight-jacket. It's useful for those starting out on a career as a storyteller. It helps aspiring writers to see what's missing in their plots and their lists of characters. I stress that it should not be followed rigidly otherwise the story will feel formulaic. It can be subverted, or it can be ignored altogether. It's a useful tool, not a non-negotiable requirement.

Another thing I've been doing with the hero's journey is showing writers how it can be used in memoirs and autobiographies for describing seasons of their lives where they face and overcome adversity. I have shown from times in my own life how I've gone through a version of the hero's journey while meeting various challenges. The hero's journey is therefore also useful in factual stories not just in fictional tales. When I came to write this book my aim was to write a medical memoir – the story of seven days of cardiac care. A memoir describes a slice of your life, not the whole of it. Writing about the whole of my life would be an autobiography. As far as I was concerned, the timeframe of my memoir was short (seven critical days), and the theme was specific (my heart - its failure and recovery). I had a seven-day plot in mind, nothing else. If I had anything deeper in my plans it was the thought that these seven days – like the seven days at the start of the Book of Genesis – might have something to do with new beginnings. Although that is what my seven-day journey became – a new start - I realised when I came to this chapter that I had unconsciously followed another plan, the hero's journey.

My experience fell into the following twelve steps:

Step 1. The Ordinary World

The hero's journey starts with the hero in their ordinary world. At this point, I need to emphasize that the word 'hero' does not necessarily refer to someone heroic. It often denotes someone ordinary who is called to something extraordinary, at least in terms of their own understanding of what constitutes their 'normal'. So, I'm not bigging myself up here. I am just saying that at the beginning of my journey I was an ordinary guy living an ordinary life. My ordinary life involved worsening ill health. This debilitated me to such a degree that I was the furthest remove from doing anything that would qualify under normal circumstances as heroic. In fact, I was incapacitated.

Step 2. The Call to Adventure

The call to adventure in my case was the diagnosis given by my local GP. "You have heart failure." This was followed by her saying that I would need to have an echocardiogram. I was to wait for a call or a text message giving me the date and time of an appointment. If I hadn't heard within three weeks, I was to get back to her. The call to adventure was therefore a call to assess the damage done to my heart and the treatment required to manage my life in the future.

Step 3. Refusal of the Call

I'm a bloke. The thing about men is that many of us engage in denial, distraction, or delaying tactics when it comes to serious health issues. In my experience, women are more like mongooses – they see a King Cobra and fearlessly attack it. Men are more like ostriches – they bury they heads in the sand. I went into ostrich mode, so much so that Cherith thought I wasn't taking things seriously. That was almost what frightened her most – not the fact that my heart had failed, but that my mind was refusing to be sufficiently concerned.

Step 4: Meeting the Mentor

Everything changed when I deteriorated on the Monday. This resulted in me heading to Maidstone for a private consultation with Doctor Edward. He turned out to be the mentor I needed to accept the call rather than refuse it. Thanks to his ECG, and his reaction to it, I soon realised that there was no time to lose and that I had to address the problems with my heart. Without Doctor Edward, there would have been no entrance into the special world of the hospital, there would have been no medical memoir, and very likely there would have been no Mark Stibbe. I was in a life-threatening state.

Step 5: Crossing the Threshold

The transition from my ordinary world (home) to a new and special world (hospital) happened the moment Cherith led me into the foyer of A&E in Ashford. The William Harvey Hospital was indeed a special world. I had never stayed overnight there. I had never had heart failure before, so I had never been a patient in a cardiac care unit. As with most such threshold experiences, there were guardians or gatekeepers – three women behind glass barriers who processed me on my arrival, assessing how urgently I needed attention. After Cherith spoke to the third one, I was triaged and then admitted.

Step 6: Tests, Allies, Enemies

There were so many tests, I don't know where to begin. The most important was the echocardiogram. This showed the full picture when it came to the failure of my heart. The allies I had in this phase of my journey were the extraordinary medical staff. They are the true heroes in our national story, as I wrote earlier. As for enemies, the greatest for us both was internal - uncertainty. We just didn't understand in layman's terms what was wrong or what the treatment plan was, not until Doctor Anne Louise walked in and explained it all.

Step 7: Approach to the Innermost Cave

There was a moment between being on the Rapid Assessment Ward and being in the Cardiac Care Unit when I was shunted into a private room in a ward that seemed to be some kind of halfway house. It was in this room that a nurse told me I needed to have a catheter fitted because I hadn't passed urine since I had arrived four hours or so earlier. I was very weak and exhausted at the time, so I had no fight in me to question this. I simply lay on my bed waiting for the procedure. I remember having to call upon my final reserves of resilience as the time for that drew nearer. I knew it would be uncomfortable and more than a little humiliating. I chose to believe it would be for the greater good of my heart, so I surrendered to the process.

Step 8: The Ordeal

It's important to emphasize that the hero's ordeal is the crisis of the story, but it is not the climax. That was true for me. I have already written about the central ordeal of my time in hospital – the fitting of the catheter, the pain I experienced several hours later, the removal, the blood, the relief. I'm wincing again even as I write this. Those were some of the worst hours of my life. Without Cherith's support, and nurse Yumi's expertise (two of my allies), this ordeal would I think have been too much for me. It was a very dark cave indeed.

Step 9: The Reward/Seizing the Sword

All these tests and trials led to Dr Anne Louise being able to tell us what we needed to hear and to lay out a pathway to getting well again. The sword we seized that Thursday lunchtime in hospital was *hope*. Both Cherith and I sensed it. We had met Anne Louise five and a half years before and we knew what qualities she possessed. She had the knowledge and authority to be our pathfinder. She lit the road ahead. We seized the sword of hope. It was going to be okay.

Step 10: The Road Back

The return to the ordinary world began on Friday morning when Dr Kevin Ward exercised his extraordinary skills and installed a turbo-charged cardiac resynchronization therapy defibrillator in my chest. The moment it was all rigged up and working, my heart started to function properly for the first time in what I think was probably decades. By the end of that Friday, this CRTD and the cocktail of meds I was being given now combined to make me feel well again. I now felt truly 'safe', to use the word Dr Edward had used on the Monday. It was at this point the medical staff started talking about me going home. It would be some time over the weekend, or on Monday. I had one foot on the road back. I was on the threshold of my ordinary world.

Step 11: Resurrection

Saturday morning, Cherith arrived for her daily visit and saw me sleeping while lying flat on my back, not sitting. It was the first time she had seen me do that in ages and she couldn't hold back the tears. I had had a brush with my mortality and lived to tell the tale. This, metaphorically speaking, was a dying and rising experience. Not only was I going to live. I looked more alive than I had done for a long time.

Step 12: Returning with the Elixir

In every story that plays out in the form of a hero's journey, the person at the heart of it returns to the ordinary world they had left behind with some kind of elixir. The word elixir denotes a healing balm or ointment. It functions as a metaphor for anything that a hero brings back from their time in the special world which brings benefit to their ordinary world. In crime thrillers, it can be truth. In adventure stories, it can be treasure. In war stories, it can be peace. In romance, it can be love. In the hero's journey, the elixir is anything that restores order, harmony, and peace to their ordinary world.

These examples point to a vital truth about the nature of the elixir. The elixir in your heroic journey can be something internal not just external, something spiritual not just material. In my case, I was in no doubt that my elixir was firstly something physical. I had a device in my chest that was enabling me to live not only longer but better. That, along with my cocktail of meds, is an NHS elixir.

Having a CRTD would have been enough in and of itself, but I returned to my ordinary with much more than just this physical benefit. There was something spiritual too.

My week in cardiac care ended on a Sunday afternoon, exactly seven days after Cherith had burst into tears while we were celebrating Gerald's restoration to health in *Clarkson's Farm*. One week later, Cherith and I left St Bartholomew after saying goodbye to the other patients and the nursing staff. Big Al was released at the same time. His wife and family made the same journey as us to the room near the hospital exit where we would sign release forms and pick up our meds for the first weeks back home. We were all in good spirits and there was a lot of laughter among us as we waited.

When Big Al and I said goodbye to each other, we both had a look in our eyes – one that said without any words, "We've been through adversity together and we are bound forever in a memory that only comes from true solidarity. We'll never forget this time together in St Bartholomew." The farewell was a strange fusion of sadness over our parting and excitement about returning home.

Cherith, of course, took charge at this stage. Last time she had driven me was the previous Monday, at high speed down the M20 from Maidstone to Ashford. Now she drove at an altogether sedater pace from Ashford to our small but picturesque village on the highest hill above and beyond the seaside town of Folkestone.

As our car pulled onto the gravel space in front of our home, I could see inside through the big glass doors. Our two painters – Colin and Wills – had moved heaven and earth to accelerate the redecoration of the interior in time for my return, but there was still a lot of furniture covered by dustsheets, as well as brushes and cans of paint stacked in little workstations around our one large room. As we entered, the smell of fresh paint filled my nostrils.

Cherith held my arm as I walked to the bedroom to see what Colin and Wills had done to get it ready. Everything felt brand new, as if the house had never been a blacksmith's forge or a holiday rental but rather, like me, a new creation. Gone were the beeping noises on the wards. All I could hear were the birds singing outside the window. And the bed! I had been in hospital beds all week, and here I was, standing at the foot of our own. To use my favourite Norwegian word, it all felt so 'koselig', an onomatopoeic word that's pronounced *kooshalee*.

I shuffled out of the bedroom to the back door a few yards away. Cherith opened it and I carefully stepped outside onto the paving slabs in front of our small garden. Under the blazing sun and bright blue skies, the grass seemed so much greener and lusher than ever before. The leaves of the bay tree on my left were in full bloom – too full, if truth be told. Two or three birds flew from the bird table beside the fence opposite where I was standing. I looked beyond the downs and towns towards the Channel and beyond these to the shores of France. As I gazed once again at the familiar landscape, as I took deep breaths and inhaled the fresh Kentish air, something unexpected happened. For the first time during this entire experience, I started to cry. At first, my eyes watered. But then the tears started to roll down my face. I was overwhelmed. I was alive. I was home. I was safe. I was hopeful. And, above all else, I was grateful.

And that's the elixir I brought back to my ordinary world - gratitude. I am more grateful than ever for the simple gift of life. Many of us may be aware of fleeting moments of gratitude in the normal course of things. It passes across the lawn of our hearts like a robin flying by in the dead of winter. We glimpse its fiery breast against the icy ground, and, for a heartbeat, we smile. But how many of us can say that our minds are everyday seized by the power of a great appreciation for the simple fact that we are alive? How many of us live in a constant spirit of thankfulness, or in what someone once called 'the gratitude attitude'? Before this journey I've been on, I know I was sometimes guilty of griping rather than gratitude. My seven days of heart failure and recovery have brought an end to that, at least for now (I cannot promise I won't ever be grumpy again!). They have offered me the chance of a new beginning, one in which I feel forever thankful.

A daily mindful state of gratitude is essential, I've now learned, for both my health and my happiness. Today I have a new perspective about what's important in life. As Daniel O'Donell, one of our favourite Irish singers, sings, "your health is your wealth." I would rather be healthy and poor than rich and sick. Being well in mind, body, and spirit is the greatest gift of all. As Irving Berlin once wrote, "Got no check books, got no banks, still I'd like to express my thanks. I got the sun in the morning and the moon at night." Amen to that!

This, then, is the elixir that I've brought back into my

ordinary world – what that great movie *A Muppet Christmas Carol* calls 'a thankful heart.' Being thankful is therapeutic. When we are grateful for a healthy life, the discipline of thanksgiving releases yet more health and life for which we can then be further thankful. This flow of gratitude is a never-ending cycle of wellbeing. And that, my friends, is the elixir. And that's what I've brought home with me.

When I was in St Bartholomew, Dr Anne Louise had come to the end of her explanation about the CRTD she wanted to have installed in my chest. She looked at Cherith and smiled. "You do realise, he could live to 150!" As Cherith smiled back, Dr Anne Louise added, "If you need me to switch him off, just ask!"

Truly, a cheerful heart is good medicine.

And a grateful heart is a great elixir.

CHAPTER 18

THIS TOO SHALL PASS

What a difference seven days had made! That first night back home I slept deep and long. I was in the same bedroom which had turned into such a battlefield in the months running up to my admission into the William Harvey Hospital. I had spent every night trying to find a position that would ease my breathlessness. I had struggled to the toilet and back more times than I could count. I think I'd single-handedly kept Kleenex Tissues and Strepsil lozenges in business. But now I was back home, all that changed. I was in bed, lying flat on my back, my breathing perfect, my bladder under control, my heart beating at a normal pace and with a synchronised rhythm.

The next morning, Cherith began her impersonation of the nurses who had looked after me so well. She brought me the pills that we had been given late the previous afternoon. After I had taken them, she took me to the scales to weigh me.

"89 kilos," she said, writing the results in her mobile phone.

"What's that in stones?"

I asked the question because I had not weighed myself for at least four years. I had been so overweight that a lawyer who had written up my case for those of us who were victims of John Smyth QC had described me as "morbidly obese." I had felt very ashamed and spiralled into a place of self-condemnation. To keep the wool over my eyes, I hadn't weighed myself since. Every time I had caught my reflection in the big mirror that used to hang in our one large room, I had convinced myself there was something wrong with the glass. It was adding pounds to my figure. I couldn't look that big, surely?

Cherith tapped on the screen of her phone.

"14 stone", she said.

I couldn't believe it. Somehow, without going to the gym or going on a diet, I had lost over 3 ½ stones. This explained a rather curious remark one of my boys had made a month before I was rushed to hospital. I had taken him out for a birthday lunch at a London restaurant. On the walk back to the railway station, we had paused to buy a coffee. I had been leaning against the counter.

"You look fit, Dad. You been training at the gym?"

I remember scratching my head.

"No, far from it."

As it happened, my lovely son was being nice to his old man. Yes, I had lost a lot of weight. No, I did not look fit. Cherith confirmed this when I had been to my local GP for the ECG five days before going to A&E, I had taken my shirt off so the nurse could apply the electrodes to my chest. When she saw me, she was horrified.

"Your arms were so thin," she recounted. "That was when I knew you were really ill."

I sat on the edge of the bed and, as I processed what I was learning about myself, Cherith put the blood pressure sleeve around my upper arm. Here again, everything was about to change. I had always shied away from having my BP checked in the past, frightened of the high reading I knew would follow. This would be anything from 150/90 to 190/100. I played the part of an ostrich with as much diligence as foolishness. In the ambulance on the way to my operation, my friendly paramedic had taken my BP, and it had read 120/80. He said this was as good as it gets. As Cherith read the results, once again the readings were, well, what Dave had called 'perfect'. I may have felt exhausted from my time in the special world of the hospital, but I was clearly doing better health wise than in a very, very long time.

Breakfast followed, and with it, further evidence of change. In hospital, all I'd wanted was a bit of porridge and a cup of tea. This was not my pre-hospital diet. I wouldn't have countenanced a cup of tea first thing in the morning. It was a very strong coffee from the Nespresso machine or my coffee pot. Anything else would not have revived me. In hospital, I developed a taste for milky tea with a teaspoon of sugar, accompanied by a bowl of porridge. The latter resembled the kind of bland and beige gruel I was served at school, but in hospital the same substance tasted like ambrosia. It's six months later and I am still sticking to this routine, although the teabags are much better at home and the porridge is made from jumbo oats. To say that my tastes have undergone a revolution is an understatement.

After breakfast, I had my first bath in over a week. I must have stunk. Cherith ran enough water so that I could lie on my back with the wound site on my chest above the surface.

"You mustn't get the wound wet during the first five days," my nurse had said.

This was followed by other instructions. "Take the dressing off after five days and give the wound a gentle clean with gauze and water. No driving for four weeks. No strenuous actions with my left arm for five weeks. The CRTD will be checked after six weeks."

After my bath, I stood in front of the mirror and looked at my chest. It was covered in red marks. These were an allergic reaction to the electrodes that had been attached to me during my stint on the wards. It took several months for these to disappear. Until they did, these and the neat but livid scar under my left collarbone made me look like I had been in a warzone. It was not a pretty sight.

There was only one thing for it and that was to rest, and for me that meant watching the bedroom TV. During my last few days in hospital, I had downloaded Pierre Boule's novel *Planet of the Apes* and listened to it through my earphones. Strange choice, I know. I loved the original Charlton Heston films in the 1960s and 70s. Maybe I was seeking to reconnect with my childhood as a means of reassurance – a kind of comfort blanket, if you will. But then my twin sister Claire wrote to me from her home in Utah:

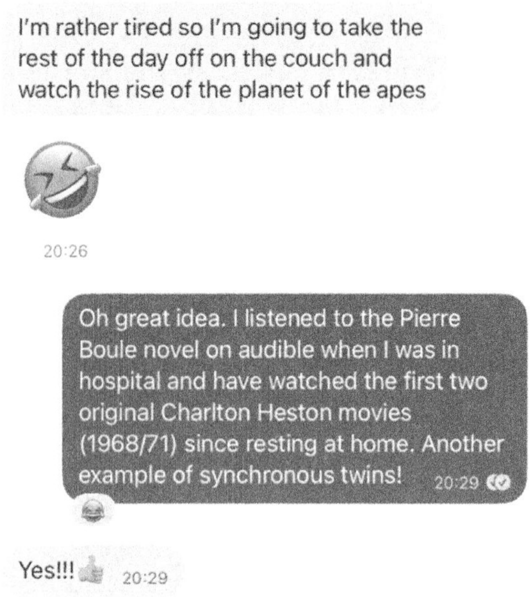

Maybe my choice was not so random!

The early *Planet of the Apes* franchise was followed by a happy discovery – all the original *Thunderbirds* episodes were available free on YouTube. So, when I wasn't napping, off my mind wandered into an equally nostalgic journey to the world of Tracy Island, Lady Penelope's English mansion, and the Evil Hood's wicked lair. I couldn't believe how well Gerry and Sylvia Anderson's show had aged. The ingenuity of the special effects was so impressive given that CGI wasn't even a twinkle in anybody's eye. The Sci-Fi gadgets used by the characters also made me shake my head in wonder; they were so prescient of today's small-screen, smart-phone technology. I remembered how much I loved Thunderbird 4 when I was a boy – you know, the underwater craft in a kind of Colman's yellow. I had always wanted a radio-controlled replica of it to play with in the bath. Now, aged 63, I searched online for an affordable model, sadly without success.

Speaking of buying things online, when I came out of surgery the previous Friday, I had told Cherith about my conversation with my surgeon about Lego. I asked her to find me the Castle of the Heron, the Lego version of the one in Japan that my surgeon had recently visited. He told me that this was the last Lego set he had bought and built. I had made an inner vow that I would do the same in his honour. Cherith, thinking that I had – in her own words – been "a brave boy in hospital", decided to go along with this idea and ordered me the set. This duly arrived, much to my excitement. When I was beginning to feel up to more than watching *Thunderbirds,* I set about the task of slowly constructing the castle. It wasn't my normal kind of build at all. I am into lighthouses and *Lord of the Rings*. But I had made a promise to myself, and I intended to keep it. Today, the Castle of the Heron is in my study. I am looking at it now. It is a constant reminder of how blessed I am and a daily prompt to be thankful.

On the medical front, my early days back home were filled with simple tasks like taking my meds (five pills at breakfast, one at midday, one early evening), being weighed, and having my BP and other vital signs measured. These results were monitored by staff in what was referred to as the *virtual hospital*. I had been released from the William Harvey and admitted onto a virtual ward on the first morning home. Staff from the William Harvey kept in regular touch with me, monitoring my results. One of the pills I was taking was a diuretic and was draining the fluid from my legs and feet, but not from my waist. Since I was deemed younger than most people with my condition, my 'virtual' nursing team decided to put me on a drug that targeted my tummy line. This it did with immediate effect. Pretty soon I was looking at the mirror and feeling almost 'beach ready'.

This phase of my recovery involved quite a lot of phone calls and a bit of tweaking (of my medication). I felt constantly cared for even though I was no longer in the physical surroundings of St Bartolomew. The attentive nurses who spoke to me in these early days couldn't do enough for me, couldn't have been kinder. Knowing that they were the other end of a phone whenever Cherith and I needed them was very reassuring. We, for our part, couldn't begin to imagine how busy they were, or what responsibilities lay upon their shoulders, so we kept our calls to the minimum, and made sure we were as polite as we were brief. These wonderful people are heroes, as I wrote in an earlier chapter. At the risk of sounding as if I'm moralising, they deserve to be treated with the greatest respect.

The first few days of recovery were therefore days of adjustment. It was all a bit strange, not least because our two friendly painters – Colin and Wills – were in our tiny house, redecorating the place. They couldn't do enough for us either.

"You alright, Mark?" Colin asked on that first Monday morning back. He looked genuinely concerned, as did his younger colleague Wills, who was taking a break from painting the bathroom.

"I'm doing fine, thanks to our wonderful NHS."

Colin nodded. He was receiving treatment too.

"Thank you for getting the bedroom ready for me coming home," I said. "I really appreciate that."

"That's alright," Wills said. "Your wife makes amazing hot drinks. She's been looking after us."

I smiled.

"I'm afraid I'll be coming through here to the loo quite a lot," I said. "It's my pills."

"That's okay," Colin said. "It's your house."

I wandered through into the bathroom and moved a few cans of paint so I could take a seat. There's no polite way of putting this, but in hospital I had found having a poo almost impossible. I mentioned earlier about my adventure with the toilet on the Rapid Assessment Ward, so you'll already know about that. Now, in the comforting surroundings of my own bathroom, I breathed a sigh of relief, and with that sigh came the great release that my now relaxed body must have been craving during the previous few days. The evacuation complete, I washed my hands and stared at my pale, tired eyes in the mirror. As I did, I became aware of the terrible odour I had produced, so I sprayed the room with deodorant, creating in the process an even worse smell of effluence and fragrance (Lidl's finest). I knew as I left the room that I was going to have to warn the two lads outside.

"In the immortal words of Alan Patridge," I said, "I wouldn't go in there for about fifteen minutes."

Colin got the reference and laughed.

Wills just looked appalled.

And so, my recovery continued. During these first few long early summer's days, I drifted in and out of sleep to the soft and comforting music played quietly and sensitively on the radio belonging to the two lads in the next-door room. Cherith continued to double up as both my private nurse and budding cook. For the previous nine years of our marriage, I had been responsible for the catering and done all the shopping, cooking, and clearing up in our cosy kitchen. Now that I was incapacitated, she had decided to sign up to *Hello Fresh* and was receiving parcels full of enticing menus and delicious ingredients for our daily main meal. I was treated to first-class cuisine every afternoon at 5pm. By the time we reached the end of the week, Colin and Wills had finished the redecorating and I was now putting on a bit of colour and much needed weight. A quotation from the pen of JRR Tolkien – my father's college professor at Merton, Oxford in the 1940s – summed up the wellbeing in my heart. “Darkness must pass. A new day will come, and when the sun shines, it will shine out the clearer.” I sent that to a few people who I knew were going through a tough time. That, and an old Persian proverb: “This too shall pass.”

Two weeks later, on May 31st, I was strong enough to visit the Cardiac Assessment Day Unit (CADU) at the William Harvey Hospital for a final checkup. I wrote the following What's App message to my boys. You can detect the gratitude in my words.

“Just to let you know I had my last visit to the hospital today and was given some final tests that all turned out very positively. I have just been phoned to say that I am formally discharged from the excellent William Harvey Hospital in Ashford. I will now be in the hands of the community heart nursing team who will be there if I need anything anytime in the future.

I am on a cocktail of meds every day from now on and of course I have the turbo defibrillator/pacemaker. I cannot speak highly enough of our wonderful NHS. Their skills and care are second to none. It is primarily due to them, and the amazing love that Cherith has shown, that I am on the mend.

Thank you for your love and prayers. I'm so grateful for you being there for me.

Just thought you'd like to know my good news."

CHAPTER 19

THE HOUNDS OF HEAVEN

Those who know me are aware of my love of animals, especially dogs. All my adult life, I have had a Black Labrador following my every move, closer to my heels than my shadow. When Cherith and I started our business coaching aspiring writers, we called it BookLab, not just because we wanted to create a laboratory where writers could innovate, but also because we share a love for Labradors. When, after decades of being published by traditional publishing houses, I decided I wanted to enjoy the freedom of self-publishing my books, we made an imprint of BookLab and called it Bella Books – after Bella, the Black Labrador who has loved us both so loyally for over ten years now. Our logo is a Black Lab. It would not be an exaggeration to say that our entire lives revolve around our dogs. Yes, we have two now. Bella, and a yellow Labrador called Phoebe, after the character in *Friends*.

One of the toughest things about being admitted to

hospital that Monday evening in Ashford was knowing that I very likely wouldn't see the dogs for a while. I work from home, so the dogs are with me every minute of every day and night. Right now, as I type, Bella is at my feet. She has been there every day while I have written many of my books – every day since she was a tiny puppy, that is. Next to her, in a bed whose material is festooned with Labradors, Phoebe – one year old – is sleeping with her back to a cushion adorned with the face of a Black Lab – a present from my mother-in-law. When we are not in the spare room which doubles up as a study, we are out twice a day on a walk in the local Kent countryside. Seeing these two creatures running through the long grass with their ears pricked and tails high always brings a smile. It's simple things that spark joy.

That Monday evening when I was in A&E with Cherith I can honestly say I was much more concerned about Bella and Phoebe being home alone than I was about my deteriorating health. I suspected that Bella could adapt to the new circumstances. With Phoebe being still a puppy, I wasn't so sure about her. When I told Cherith, she phoned two friends of ours, Saul and Rachel, who run a very busy and popular vintage clothes shop in our local town (*Bounce*, in Folkestone). Like true friends, they dropped everything and headed straight to our house. They let themselves in and took the dogs for a walk. When they had fed and settled them, they tucked them up in bed, left quietly, and sent us some photos and a message. I cannot begin to tell you how reassured that made me feel. I could relax now, knowing that Cherith would be back home sometime later that night, and that they would be okay at least until the next day. The next day, however, brought a new challenge. By now I had been admitted, and it was clear that I would be in hospital for a while. Ten days was mentioned.

"What about the dogs?" I asked Cherith.

"I'll call Kerry."

Let me tell you about Kerry. Kerry is one of the most beautiful souls we have ever met. She owns a house in the same county as us about fifteen minutes away from where we live. Cherith would say that her home is her dream house because it's designed for looking after animals, especially dogs. It's secured by an impenetrable system of fences and contains an area behind the house where dogs can run and play. Some of these dogs belong to her, but most are in her care for a few days or weeks. This is because Kerry looks after other people's dogs for a living. She used to be a copper on the beat in Folkestone, but decided – quite understandably in my humble opinion – that dogs are nicer than most human beings, so she resigned from the force and set up a small business as a professional dog carer. And she's brilliant at it. Both our dogs love staying with her. They go mad with joy when we drop them off, and they go mad with joy when we pick them up – which, speaking for myself, is how you want it as a dog owner.

Putting two dogs in Kerry's care for up to ten days was not going to be cheap, but it was going to be worth it, not just for our peace of mind, but for theirs too. It's hard to imagine them being looked after better anywhere else this side of heaven. That's why they're as giddy as kids going to a sleepover when we tell them, "You're going to stay with Auntie Kerry." Nothing is guaranteed to cause Bella's big tail to start wagging more wildly than mentioning staying with Kerry. She knows exactly what we mean, and Phoebe – seeing Bella in euphoric mood – copies her mentor and starts getting excited too.

That Monday morning in hospital, when Cherith arrived at the Rapid Assessment Ward bearing a Costa coffee, my first question was of course about the dogs.

"I phoned Kerry just after 6.30am," she said. "I told her what was going on with your heart and she told me to bring them over. I've just dropped them off at her house."

"But how long can she have them?"

"She said as long as we need."

This was one of the many moments during these challenging days when I felt utterly overwhelmed by the kindness of our family, friends, and medical staff. I think dogs are great, yes. But I also think that human beings are capable of greatness too.

"Kerry's amazing," Cherith said as she passed me my coffee.

"She's a saint," I said.

For the next few days, I was able to devote myself to getting the help I needed, something I could do without distraction now that I knew the dogs were in the best possible hands. When I returned home the following Sunday, Cherith and I agreed that the dogs would be far too excited and that I would be too frail. Phoebe would want to jump up and lick me, putting the wound site on the left side of my chest in jeopardy. The wound needed time to heal, and I needed time to build my strength and confidence. I was a little scared that I didn't have enough muscle to protect myself against a leaping Labrador.

We came home Sunday night, but it wasn't until

Wednesday afternoon that we drove over to Kerry's house to pick up the girls. By then, I was feeling a bit more robust, and my anxieties had been replaced by an eagerness to be reunited.

When we parked up and closed the gates, Kerry appeared from the back garden. She gave me a gentle hug and said how pleased she was to see me back in the land of the living.

The next moment, the dogs appeared. Seeing them again was one of the most joyful moments of my life.

And I needn't have worried about them being overexcited. They both seemed to know I was frail. Maybe it was the way I looked, or walked, but they didn't jump. They just wanted to be close. And when we came home after one of Kerry's brilliant brews, all they wanted to do was lie on the bed with me while I watched *Thunderbirds*. They were clearly exhausted from ten days in the company of other dogs, going for two long walks a day, and no doubt up to all sorts as they slept dormitory-style with other dogs at night.

That first Wednesday evening back together, Cherith sent a WhatsApp message to Kerry, asking how much we owed her. We were bracing ourselves for quite a hefty bill. Two dogs for ten days and nights in the Canine Savoy was not going to be cheap. I needn't have worried about that. When Kerry's answer came back a few minutes later, it moved us both to tears. She wasn't going to accept any money. Knowing that I was on the mend was payment enough.

There are some truly amazing people in this world.

I needn't have worried about Phoebe either. Yes, she is a puppy. Yes, she is crazy sometimes. But she knew I was not in a state for the normal rough-and-tumble play. They say that the heart of a dog synchronizes with the heart of its owner. If there's any truth in that, Phoebe would have known that my heart needed tender loving care. And she did know. One afternoon, Cherith was filming Phoebe and me on her phone. I was sitting in my pyjamas on the sofa. Phoebe was sitting beside me, leaning against the right side of my body. While Cherith was filming us, Phoebe leaned her head very gently on my heart and started to lick my T-shirt directly over where my heart – now resynchronized by my amazing surgeon – was beating. We posted that ten-second video on Facebook. The response was phenomenal. People could not believe how empathetic dogs are.

Then came the biggest challenge of all.

The first walk.

Cherith had been walking the girls instead of me – twice every day for weeks. This had been great while she was allowed compassionate leave from work, but this was only going to last so long. I was going to need to get back into the routine, if not for the dogs' sake, for the sake of my own fitness and health. Cherith and I took the plunge and took the dogs for a truncated version of the usual walk around the local fields. Normally, this involves a hill, but I wasn't yet confident enough to take that on, so we cut that part out and kept on level ground. I managed the whole thing just fine. No breathlessness. No fatigue. I felt energised by the bright sunshine and exhilarated by the familiar countryside. Within a few weeks, I had built up enough miles to take on the hill. I managed it better than I ever had. Cherith was with me. She realised that it was safe for me now to be let out on my own.

What happened next was remarkable. One midweek afternoon in June, when Cherith was back at her desk in Canterbury, I took the dogs out on our usual walk, including descending and ascending the inclines. I was about to rejoin the road that led back home when I saw someone walking towards me with two shaggy dogs. I was slightly surprised because I rarely saw anyone else there. I had taken this walk for almost six years. I could count on my fingers the times I had met anyone. I had certainly never passed the person that was now approaching me. At twenty metres, I recognised her.

Dr Anne Louise!

In front of me was the woman whose dogged

determination (pardon the pun) had secured an outside defibrillator for the parish and an internal defibrillator for my heart.

On the first walk on my own, on a track where I never met anyone else – and certainly not Anne Louise – I bump into my heart doctor! What are the chances of that?

"It's nice to see you in your normal clothes," she said.

I made some feeble remark about being in one of those one-piece gowns the last time she had seen me – the ones that don't do up properly around the back.

"That's why we call it ICU," she said.

It took a moment for my still rather weary brain to get the joke, but when I did, I laughed.

That wasn't the last time I laughed either. A few weeks later, I was having a cup of tea on a Sunday morning when the dogs started getting excited. Their hackle was up as they stared out into the garden. Looking through the window, I saw what they were barking at - a peacock. That was a first for us. We've seen pheasants, woodpeckers, and even owls in our garden, but never a peacock.

Then I remembered something. Dr Anne Louise and her husband looked after peacocks!

Realising I had her number in our community group on my phone (from lockdown days), I texted her. It turned out one of her peacocks had gone missing - one with a broken head feather. Anne Louise wrote, "He looks as if he's had a jolly night out!!!" Eventually he left and Anne Louise sent a photo of him with the caption, "He's home!" She didn't hold out much hope that he would stay there. She added, "But he'll probably drop by yours. Later..."

To this day, these moments intrigue me. I've written

about synchronicity earlier. For some, these will be examples of "the universe" at work. But the word universe is not personal enough for me. I prefer to think in terms of providence, and of love at work. Divine love. The love that watches out for us. Which brings me back to dogs. I have always seen the unconditional love of a dog as an apt analogy for the love of God. The great reformer Martin Luther once remarked that "The dog is the most faithful of animals and would be much esteemed were it not so common. Our Lord God has made his greatest gift the commonest." For those who prefer something a little less Protestant, then here's a Native American proverb: "God Made the earth, the sky and the water, the moon and the sun. He made man and bird and beast. But He didn't make the dog. He already had one."

During my recovery, our two dogs have constantly reminded me of the ever-faithful love of God. That love leans on my heart daily, kissing it back to health and life.

What then of the wandering peacock? What is this supposed to signify? Nothing really. All I can say is that the peacock was a bald old boy who found himself in a strange environment for a while before finding his way home.

A bit like me, then.

So, maybe he's a simple reminder that human beings are not as different from animals after all and that we are all more connected than we sometimes realise.

God's creatures played a big part in my early days back home, especially our dogs. They reminded me that someone or something has been watching out for me, for us, all along.

And in case you're still not convinced, one final story. When we next took the dogs to Kerry, she got her diary out when we talked about further dates for the dogs to stay.

"It was so strange when you were in hospital," she remarked.

"What was?"

"Well, your girls were here for ten days."

She opened her diary at the dates.

"In the run up to that Monday, it was chocker here.

I couldn't have taken them. And in the days after that Wednesday when they left, I would have been too full too. Those were literally the only the days they could have come here."

Funny that, isn't it?

It's almost as if there was a plan.

CHAPTER 20

A DIFFERENT PACE

Looking back on my life before my time in hospital, I can remember occasions when my heart seemed 'off'. Even when I was a little boy, I can recall it beating fast and loud. I would sometimes lie on my side in bed with my ear pressed against my pillow. I would listen to the beat of my heart, and it seemed to be racing, sometimes thumping. Occasionally, it felt as if the beat wasn't in time. All this I shrugged off, not just as a child, but as a teenager, and then as a grown man. *It must be normal*, or that at least was what I figured.

Having been hospitalised, I now realise it was far from that. I am due to have an appointment soon at the Royal Brompton Hospital in London. It will be interesting to learn how long they think I've had this condition, and whether it's something I inherited. As an adopted child, I don't know my cardiac family history.

One thing I do now know with some certainty is the reason why I lived so much of my life at an unhealthily accelerated pace. At the wedding service for my first marriage, the officiating minister was Maurice Wood, the then bishop of Norwich. His family and mine knew each other well. My father was headteacher of Norwich School, based in the Cathedral Close in Norwich. The headteacher's house was in the Close too, as was the bishop's residence. This meant that we all saw a fair bit of each other. In addition, the bishop and I shared a love for the Canaries. He had a seat in the director's box at Carrow Road and when he sponsored me for ordination, he invited me to join him there. I always enjoyed his company. He had a great sense of humour, and was a straight-talking and, on occasions, blunt cleric.

The wedding day furnished a good example. He decided to preach a sermon based on my namesake Gospel, Mark, and on one word for which Mark the storyteller had a particular fondness. In the original Greek text of this Gospel the word is *eutheus*, which means 'immediately.' Mark uses this over 40 times which is one reason why the pace of this Gospel narrative seems so quick. For example, Peter and Andrew "immediately" leave their nets to follow Jesus. When Jesus raises Jairus's dead daughter, he "immediately" takes her by the hand. The bishop used this brief textual insight as the launchpad for describing me, another man called Mark, as "a man in a hurry." He gave examples of my obvious impatience in a semi-scolding tone, then turned into full-on didactic discourse, cautioning me against being impatient in my marriage. I didn't heed his advice. I lived at breakneck speed for the next thirty years until my divorce. My pace of life was out of control. Maybe part of this was because I wanted to distract myself from the serious fault lines in the marriage itself. But maybe also it was because I was dancing to the beat of a manic drum.

Think about it. If your heart is thumping fast and irregularly, the chances are that's how you're going to live. It's like one of those old-school movies. You know the ones. There's a Roman galley and there are oarsmen below deck. The drummer, the slavedriver, is beating a big drum, and the oarsmen are picking up the pace when he does. Their behaviour is dictated by his beat. The harder he hits the canvas, the more they pull on their oars. If you've seen *Ben Hur* (1959), you've watched Charlton Heston and his fellow slaves accelerating from "battle speed" to "attack speed" and then to "ramming speed" in response to the drummer's beat. In all this, the invisible percussionist is the determining factor in their visible performance.

I don't think that's a bad analogy at all for how I was living. During my first marriage, and the roughly identical years I spent as an ordained priest in the Church of England, I worked harder and harder to achieve the goals I set for myself. Towards the end, in a futile attempt to give my family a standard of living that I felt they deserved, I was not only vicar of one of the largest churches in the country, I was also travelling throughout the UK and abroad speaking at conferences, and I was writing several books a year. This was an unsustainable pace. My heart was already at "battle" speed. It's just I didn't know it.

After my divorce, the problems with my heart began to become a little more obvious. One night, I had a terrible allergic reaction to something I ate. I had never had an allergic reaction to anything before, nor have I since, and if you ask me what it was that caused it, I cannot give you a clear answer. But the effect of all this was that Cherith drove me to the William Harvey Hospital, to their A&E department – not for the last time, as you can see from this book. There the doctor noticed I had very high blood pressure. He told me to go to my GP and have it checked. With Cherith's persuasion, I agreed.

An examination at my local surgery revealed that I was suffering from dangerous levels of hypertension. To use the language of *Ben Hur*, I had somehow managed to accelerate from battle speed to attack speed. In other words, if I didn't take medication, I was in danger of suffering from a heart attack or a stroke. I was duly put on tablets for high BP. The dose was increased from 5mg to 10mg a day when it became clear that the initial prescription was not enough. I was supposed to be called into the surgery once every year to have a blood test to assess whether this prescription was working effectively, and whether there were any negative side effects, particular in my kidneys. Somehow, this was never activated, so by the time I went to my doctor with symptoms of heart failure ten years later, she looked at my records on her screen and declared with surprise, "Where are your bloods?"

I was an accident waiting to happen.

A galley at ramming speed.

A crash was imminent and inevitable.

When I went to A&E with acute heart failure, I was told there are two ways in which this kind of crash can happen to you. The first is sudden. I'm talking about a heart attack. The second is gradual. I'm talking about your heart slowly functioning with less and less energy. The ECGs and blood tests I had in A&E that Monday night revealed that I was suffering from the second, and that if I did not say yes to being admitted and treated, I was in danger of experiencing the first. So, I entered hospital and four days later Dr Kevin Ward inserted my CRTD – my cardiac re-synchronization therapy defibrillator – after I had started a course of medication. The two in combination had an immediate effect. Not only did they reduce most of the symptoms I had been enduring. They synchronised the chambers of my heart and produced a regular rhythm.

When I think about this, I marvel at our interconnectedness at an individual level. We truly are composed of a body, mind, and spirit (BMS). I have devoted a lot of time in the past to this triunity, but what I never saw was the connection between the pacing of my heart and the pacing of my life. I had always understood the way beliefs (your mind) affect your behaviour (your body), but what I had never understood was the way something as fundamental as your heartbeat and heart rate (your body) affects your decisions about the pace at which you live your life (your mind). As Ralph Waldo Emerson once said, "Adopt the pace of nature; her secret is patience."

How do I know that this connection even exists? The answer has to do with the speed and rhythm of my heart both before and after my time in hospital. On her first day visiting me on the wards, Cherith had left home after the painters arrived. She told them that I was in hospital suffering from heart failure.

"I thought he was *pacing* a bit when I saw him."

These words were uttered by Colin, the older of our two decorators. He and I had met very briefly the previous week. I had been standing in the kitchen doing some clearing up when we were chatting. As far as I was concerned, I was acting normally. I was operating at my regular speed just doing some household chores. But Colin told Cherith that he thought I was *pacing*, a word I had never heard used in that way before, and certainly never of me.

Today, this choice of words still strikes Cherith and me as very significant, very telling. To my mind, the word not only denotes acceleration; it also conveys the idea of frustration, as in "pacing about". Clearly there was something in my demeanour and behaviour that raised red flags in Colin's mind. My *pacing* was not right, so my trip to A&E to him at least was no great surprise.

And it shouldn't have been a surprise to me either. For a very long time – right back into childhood - I had experienced moments that could now, looking back, be described as cautionary. I'm referring to those times when I knew the pacing of my heart was strange – those instants when the beat was too loud and fast, the rhythm not synchronized and smooth. I chose to leave that drumbeat in the background, not realising that it was driving me at breakneck speed – like Charlton Heston and his crew – towards ever-increasing danger.

Not anymore.

After I came out of hospital, everything changed. I started living life at a different pace. I slowed down not just in body, but in mind and spirit too. Let me give you an example. Before my lifechanging treatment, I was a bit of a pain every time Cherith and I went out for a meal or a meeting. I would get more and more cranky the nearer we got to what I regarded as the estimated time of departure. I would say things like "five-minute warning", which Cherith would then parrot back to me in act of dismissive parody.

We would nearly always be late getting into the car, and I would try and make up time in the way I drove. All very unhealthy in hindsight.

Today, I am very different. For example, when we decided to fly to Northern Ireland and see Cherith's wonderful family and friends, we nearly missed our flight. This situation arose because when it was time to leave home and drive to the airport, instead of me doing my normal thing and counting down the clock, I sat and watched YouTube in the sitting room. Cherith, who was expecting the normal "five-minute warning," heard nothing as she calmly straightened her hair in the next-door room. When I realised that we were late leaving, instead of behaving like a Formula One racing driver, I drove us at a leisurely pace to Gatwick and then strolled to the gate.

We only just made it.

That kind of behaviour was inconceivable before my CRTD was inserted in May 2024. That device really has proven to be a pacemaker. It has produced a healthy pace for my heart, and it has created a healthy pace for my life. I move at a very different tempo now. I am no longer a man in a hurry. I am slowing down, appreciating every passing moment, pausing to look around and allow the little things to satisfy my curiosity and evoke a sense of wonder.

When I try to analyse why I was the way I was, I know that this was in part to do with the rhythm of my heart, but I think there was something else, not unrelated to that, and that's to do with time. I believe it was Eleanor Roosevelt who once said that "yesterday is history, tomorrow is a mystery, but today is a gift, that's why it's called the present." In my case, I think my accelerated pace was not just due to the beating of my inner drum. It was due to a wrong belief that the present wasn't important; it was tomorrow that really mattered. I was a driven man, striving to earn love through achieving success. In that respect, I was living the life of a slave, hurrying to enter a better future. I believed the lie that the end of some mythical rainbow was just around the corner. There I would find my field of gold. When I began my treatment for heart failure, I had a complete sea change in my thinking. Overnight, I stopped being driven towards some putative future. I chilled out and started to enjoy the gift that is the present. In short, instead of behaving like a slave, I started behaving like a son. Instead of working *for* rest, I started working *from* rest – the rest that comes from knowing that I am a human being more than I am a human *doing*, and that the simple act of being is of infinite value. To use the words of Robert Louis Stevenson, I now have a quiet mind that proceeds at its own "private pace, like a clock during a thunderstorm."

In the months after I came out of hospital, I have been back three times to have my CRTD checked. This involves having a sensor placed over my heart. The nurse on duty checks that all three leads from the CRTD are operating at maximum efficiency. This requires her adjusting the settings on her laptop, resulting in changes in my heart. She can basically make my heart go faster or slower, depending on what she's trying to change in the operating efficiency of the leads she's monitoring. If I didn't trust her 100%, it would be a scary and uncomfortable ride. She has complete control of my cardiac functions. If she were Nurse Ratchet, I'd be a goner.

The last time I went, the nurse – Lauren – asked if I had

ever heard the alarm on my CRTD.

"No one's ever told me I had one," I replied.

"We often get that," she said. "It's the one thing we always seem to forget to tell our patients. Would you like to hear yours?"

I nodded.

A few seconds later, I heard what sounded like the siren of a distant ambulance. It was quiet, more of a background noise than the loud alert I was expecting.

"When that goes off," Lauren said, "you need to contact the clinic straightaway. It means the device needs checking."

She switched off the alarm and looked at me.

"You want to hear a funny story?"

"Of course!"

"We had an elderly chap with a pacemaker and his alarm went off while he was lying in bed with his wife. He couldn't work out where the sound was coming from. He and his wife searched all over their house. They even cleared out their attic before they eventually realised it was him, or more accurately, his pacemaker."

I laughed.

Laughter seemed to accompany our visits to hospital during those recovery months. Recently, I made my way back to William Harvey early one morning for a PET-CT scan. Before entering what looked like an enormous Polo mint, I was given a radioactive injection and asked to sit still for an hour. The substance was designed to help the imaging team see more clearly what was going on mainly in my heart and lungs. During my prepping, I was politely informed by the nursing staff not to use the toilet in the foyer of the PET-CT Scan building after my procedure. "There's a special WC in the corridor outside the scanning room. It's designed for radioactive patients." This explained the warning I'd seen on the public loo in the waiting area.

That made us laugh too.

Before I conclude, I should share with you the results of all my scans. What they have revealed is this: I have a very unusual heart condition known as cardiac sarcoidosis. No, I hadn't ever heard of that before either. Here's a useful definition I found online: "cardiac sarcoidosis is a rare disease in which your body's immune response to inflammation makes scars. These harm your heart, causing abnormal heart rhythms. Scars can get in the way of heartbeat signals, keeping them from getting where they need to go. Most people need medication, but others need devices to keep their hearts beating normally." Cardiac sarcoidosis is a disease that afflicts very few people. In fact, the number is so small that my heart doctor knows of only one unit which specialises in it in the UK – a cardiac sarcoidosis clinic at the Royal Brompton Hospital (London, UK). Only 250 patients a year are referred there from all over the world. That's a tiny number! I'll be heading there before too long to get some advice about next steps.

Anyway, back to the issue of pacing yourself. Just as people like Lauren monitor the pacing of my heart, I'm responsible for monitoring the pacing of my life. Something my brother Giles said to me has helped with that. He encouraged me to live my life by the ancient motto, *festina lente*, which means "hurry slowly" in Latin. That's an oxymoron, but I think I get what it means. Before I had my cardiac care, it was just *festina* – hurry. Now, the word *lente* has been added, so I hasten slowly. I can still do things with a sense of urgency, but my slower and quieter internal rhythm means that I now do them with less drivenness, less impatience. All this has taught me that the greatest obstacle to true inner health is uncontrolled 'hurrying.' We must learn to hurry slowly, and to do that we must allow our hearts to set a different pace, a different rhythm, otherwise we do ourselves great harm.

This morning, I lay on my side in bed during the dawn's early light. I pressed my ear against my pillow and listened to the pace and rhythm of my heart. It was no longer loud like before, but quiet. No longer fast, but slow. No longer irregular, but constant.

Festina lente I whispered to myself, as the birds trilled outside the window and our yellow Lab snored at my feet.

Festina lente.

EPILOGUE: A PARTNER'S EXPERIENCE

Cherith and I were having lunch recently with two friends, Neil and Lynda. Lynda has been supporting her husband Neil through years of cancer treatment. When I shared that I was writing this book, Lynda asked, "Are you going to have anything from the partner's point of view - anything about the experience of what it's like caring for your loved one in a time like this?" I hadn't thought of that, but it seemed like the perfect way to finish this memoir. So, here's the transcript of an interview Cherith gave about her time watching me go through my ordeal and supporting me as we navigated an unfamiliar medical landscape together.

What were things like for you before Mark's diagnosis with heart failure?

It started off with us being convinced that Mark had a bad cold. Eventually, it got bad enough for him to go to the doctor. He was told he had a chest infection, so that's what we thought it was. I didn't at the time doubt that. But it wasn't until the antibiotics for the chest infection didn't work that I started to get concerned. I thought the antibiotics would have hit it, but they didn't. He started to get more and more tired, and not functioning at all. I remember seeing him sit out the back of the house with his mouth open, and it was like he didn't even have the energy to keep his mouth closed. That was scary. That was on the Sunday, a couple of days after he had been diagnosed with heart failure.

Let's talk about that diagnosis. What was it like hearing from the doctor that Mark had heart failure?

When I heard the words 'heart failure', I was worried. I went through so many emotions very quickly. I think the doctor must have seen the anxiety in my face because she added, "but often this can be treated with medication." I was processing so many things all at once. I knew he had been seriously unwell, but then she was being quite positive. And then, when we came out of the doctors, Mark gave me a big hug and said, "I'm so relieved." My head was spinning at this point. Part of me didn't understand why he was feeling that way. But then part of me did, because we had been surrounded by people whose loved ones had received a terminal diagnosis of cancer.

Do you think at this stage you and Mark had a different perspective on what was going on?

Yes. I remember going back to work and phoning my mum on the way. I took the positive line. "It's heart failure, but it's going to be okay. It's all good. The doctor seemed very positive." But then I started googling stuff. Someone I worked with at the time said to me that day, "Are you okay?" I said yes. Months later, she said she knew I hadn't been. The things I was seeing on Google about symptoms meant that

I realised that things were a lot more serious and advanced than Mark did. I thought, *I think he's further along this road than we'd like him to be.*

What happened then to make everyone realise just how serious this was?

It was when we were told that Mark wasn't likely to have an echocardiogram for some weeks, maybe months, that I became concerned because I didn't think we had that amount of time. I didn't want to think it was that serious, but I did. By this time, my mum had already mentioned that if things were taking too long, she and Dad would pay for a private consultation. At that private appointment, there was still a huge part of me that wanted Dr Edward to say, "Yes, this is what it is, but we can treat it with medication, and everything's going to be okay." But that's not what happened. Things accelerated very quickly after Doctor Edward examined him. He ordered an ECG. During that, his demeanour changed. I could tell that he was concerned. When he said, "He's got to go to A&E," something switched in me. I went straight into action mode. That was the turning point for me. Then I thought, *There's no petrol in the car!* I hadn't ever thought we'd end up in A&E. I thought the consultation would speed up the process of Mark having the echocardiogram. I thought we'd probably have to pay. It would probably be next week. Mark would probably be resting at home until then, maybe with some advice about coping, and some meds. When Doctor Edward said we had to go, I thought, *Right, let's get this done.* I knew where the petrol station was, so I drove there. When I turned in to get petrol, I remember just saying thank you audibly to

God. The relief I felt was overwhelming, knowing that it wasn't in my hands anymore, it wasn't my responsibility. I knew nothing about Mark's condition. I knew if there were solutions, they would now be found.

What did you have to do to get Mark seen?

I remember parking in a space reserved for ambulances so I could drop him off at A&E. I parked the car in the right place after I had sat him down in A&E. Dr Edward had given me a letter about Mark's condition and I naively thought this would be like a passport, getting him straight into a cardiac ward. But that's not what happened. So, the letter helped, but it didn't speed things up in the way I imagined. I had to push more than I thought I would. So, for the first couple of hours, I felt stressed, before I got to a point when I thought, *You're in A&E. He's in the system. They have his name. They have the letter. Even if anything happens at this point – like he has a heart attack – he's in the right place. I need to put my trust in these people and just pray that everything works out the way it needs to.*

I think we'd all agree that when it comes to couples, one can sometimes be pushy while the other can be passive. Does that accurately describe your relationship?

[Laughter] When it comes to medical things, I would be the active one, but then Mark didn't have the energy to do anything even had he wanted to. He was too weak. Concentrating on pure survival. I was directing a lot of my energy into not showing that I was feeling stressed because I didn't want to put any more pressure on his failing heart.

So, what was the hardest thing after that?

After about six hours, I had to go home to fetch some things for Mark – toiletries, pyjamas, and the like, and the thing that I found hardest about that was not so much being away from him – he was in the safest place – but seeing the dogs at home. I thought to myself that I couldn't break down because I couldn't have them freaking out because I was upset. There was a very small part of me which I didn't allow to take hold that was saying, "I don't know if I'm ever going to walk into our home with him again..." [tears]. That was in me, but I refused to let it out because I had to be strong. The girls [two Labradors] looked to see where he was. They were okay until the next morning when Phoebe [our yellow Labrador puppy] was upset because he wasn't there. She was behaving oddly. But after that, I developed a routine going home. I would have a shower, something to eat, a couple of hours sleep, and then I'll go back. That was the focus.

What did you experience during the week he was in hospital?

I had a laser-sharp focus on making sure that he was being looked after properly, which I needn't have worried about because the medical staff were amazing. There was nothing else in the world going on for me other than that. Everything else was gone. The only time I struggled was that dark Wednesday when he was in the Cardiac Care Unit. That was because he was upset and I had never in our relationship seen him like that. It was a really different dynamic to our normal. He's always the strong one. Always steadfast. If I'm upset, he's very measured. He was so vulnerable that day. I was really struggling in that moment and the person

I always go to, 100% of the time, is him, but I couldn't do that because I had to support him. That was really hard because he was so upset. So, I called my mum. She's a very good balance of compassion and realism. She told me to look at the facts. "Has anyone actually said that this is looking bleak? Have any of the staff used any words that have given you any cause to believe that?" I said no. She then added, "Doctors nowadays will be brutally honest, so if they haven't said that, then this is good." That was the only day I cried when he was in hospital. But I came back from that when I talked with Mum.

You talk about Wednesday being a very dark day, what happened to change that?

I'll never forget on Thursday Dr Anne Louise walking into the ward. She was just so clear. So decisive. She knew what was wrong with Mark's heart and she knew what likely needed to happen as a solution. She just needed to check his arteries, so she ordered an angiogram for later that same day. Most of all, she was so clear about the treatment plan. That was the first time that we realised there was a treatment plan. Up until then, we didn't know. Or if there was any hope at all. But now hope came into the equation. I always had faith. But not hope – at least medical hope. But because she was so confident, and so easy to understand, I thought that this was amazing and that she was incredible. Then there was her little aside, "I'm your neighbour." My head began to spin, but not in a negative way this time. It had been negative spinning when we got the diagnosis – with our GP, and with Dr Edward. This time it was positive. Really positive. We don't live in a big village. Our population is just over 40. So, the fact that it was our neighbour standing there felt really meant.

Were you worried while Mark was in surgery on the Friday?

Yeah, I was. I had to do stuff so as not to think about it. I didn't have the dogs at this stage. They were with Kerry. If they'd still been at home, I'd have taken them for a walk as a distraction. So, I went into work to pick up a laptop and talk to colleagues. That was helpful, because it was like stepping back in time to before anything had ever happened. This was my 'life before'. I went into that mode. I was there for a little while. I couldn't have asked for better in terms of support from my work. One night after I had visited Mark, I phoned my line manager, Julia, just to update her and to check I was going to get paid. I was so out of it that I didn't realise it was 9pm and that this wasn't very sensitive. I was on the phone to her for about half an hour. She was genuinely concerned. She applied absolutely no pressure. They could not have been better. So, I got something to eat. Picked up some stuff from the shops for when he came home. I went to the Range to get him a special pillow for sitting up in bed, and a portable table for him to eat meals while he was recuperating. I just made sure that I was always doing something.

What do you remember of Mark coming home on Sunday?

I remember him getting into the car and feeling so, so grateful. I had driven that car so much that week and there had been a little part of me that never knew if we'd ever be in the car together again, but I didn't allow myself to go there. I remember him just sitting beside me and feeling just so grateful... [tears]... that he was with me again... [tears] that everything was going to be okay. He had been through so much, but there were too many things that had happened, too many little coincidences which told me that he was meant to be where he was, that I knew everything was going to be alright.

What were the challenges of effectively having to nurse him over the following weeks and months?
Coming out of hospital I was nervous because 24/7 he had been monitored, attached to various devices. They were keeping an eye on him all the time. I found it scary that they weren't going to be there even though his body was presumably going to be doing the same sorts of things that they had been dealing with. But then when Mark was set up as a patient with the virtual hospital, I still felt like we had the support of the professionals we needed.

What was it like seeing his scars, and knowing he had a device in his chest keeping him alive?
Honestly, the only word I can think of is gratitude. Even still, when I see that scar ... [tears] ... I just think. 'Thank you.' If he didn't have that scar, he wouldn't be here. So, I love that scar so much [laughter], which is such a weird thing to say, but I just know that if it wasn't there, then he wouldn't be either.

Were there any other specific challenges?
When I knew he was coming home, I thought, "Oh my

gosh! I haven't cooked in about ten years! He's a proper, like, chef. He cooks amazing stuff. I can't serve him up my s**t! Also, he really needs to be eating healthily. So, I signed up to Hello Fresh and they were a Godsend. That wasn't really a challenge in the end, because of them.

What about the reunion with the dogs?
That was the thing I was looking forward to most. That was one of the most emotional moments because that first night I came home to them from the hospital I just didn't know if I was ever going to see Mark again, so to go to Kerry's house and to watch them was amazing. It was a normal reaction in one respect, because whenever we leave them with Kerry, they are so excited, but when we pick them up, they are really excited as well. From their perspective, it was a normal pickup, if you get what I mean. But it's one of those things that when you go through an experience like that, the things that used to be normal become incredible and beautiful. You just want to live in that moment forever. They were so excited, and yet gentle too. I was concerned that Phoebe would go mad when she saw Mark and jump all over him, but she didn't. She was thrilled but she was calm, muted a little bit. They could tell he was weak and that they needed to be careful, and she was. Then there was that moment when we were home. It was a few weeks later. Mark was sitting on the sofa feeling a bit rough emotionally about what this all meant for him, and Pheobe climbed up next to him, leant her head on his chest, and started sniffing around his heart, and then licked his T shirt exactly where his heart is. I have never seen anything like it.

Do you now see a difference in Mark's attitude towards going to the doctor, to hospital, and so on?

Yes. Mark is a person who's very much focused on other people, so he would tend to say that he was okay because he wouldn't want anyone to be worried or upset. Whereas if I had been exhibiting the symptoms he had been suffering, he would have been telling me to get myself to the doctor. Now he's much more acutely aware of things he needs to keep an eye on, see a GP about, report to his heart nurse, or his heart doctor. He's much better at listening to his body. If he's tired, he'll rest. This is something his heart doctor Ann told him. It sounds a bit cheesy, but listening to his body has proven to be the perfect advice for his recovery. People should be listening to their bodies all the time and paying more attention to changes, not in a kind of hypochondriac way, but being aware is big.

And finally, how important has your faith been in the whole experience?

It has been everything. All those moments that I don't even think you can see as a coincidence... Anne Louise turning up. Little things too. But those little things got me through that week. The best way I can describe it is that I felt held. Someone was holding me up. I remember when Mark was having his pacemaker fitted and I was driving the car, I was listening to hymns and songs. They weren't ones I had chosen, but some of them were just perfect for that moment. So specific. Songs about giving God your heart. You could see that as coincidence, but I very much don't. God was there and was walking with us through it. I'm sure of it. So, faith was everything.... *is* everything.

ACKNOWLEDGEMENTS

I'm so grateful to Esther Kotecha for the cover design, typesetting, and formatting of this book, to my wife Cherith for her editing work and for her immensely helpful suggestions for changes, and finally to Grant Matcham and Julian Campbell for their careful reading of the proofs. I continue to be deeply thankful for all the support and expertise I receive from others. Publishing a book like this is truly a team effort. Promoting it is too. With that in mind I would like to thank Jimmy and Edie for offering their cosy bar at Remedies on the high street in Hythe, Kent, for the launch of this book.

ABOUT THE AUTHOR

Mark has been writing books since he was 16 and has clocked up over 50 titles. Some of his early titles were academic works. For example, his PhD on storytelling was completed in 1982 and subsequently published by Cambridge University Press. Most of his books in the years after that were, until recently, religious nonfiction. Mark was a Church of England vicar for over twenty years and served in four parishes, two as a curate, two as a vicar.

Having been an adopted child, much of Mark's work has focused on what he calls 'the healing of the orphan heart'. He feels passionate about setting people free from the effects of abandonment and abuse suffered during their time at boarding school. His book *Home at Last: Freedom from Boarding School Pain* (2015) has proven helpful to many wounded ex-boarders. A new title, *The Broken Bond. Boarding School and the Mother Wound* has been commissioned for 2026.

In 2015, Mark started writing novels for the mass market. *A Book in Time* was picked as the overall winner in the Page Turner Award for Fiction Writing in 2020. His latest novel is *Dead Man Talking* – the first in a series of supernatural thrillers, this one a WW2 story about racial discrimination. At the same time, Mark continues to write nonfiction. *Fathers: the Top Seven Dad Skills*, won the General Nonfiction Award at the New York Book Festival in 2023.

As a victim of John Smyth QC – dubbed the Church of England's Jimmy Saville – Mark has campaigned on mainstream media on behalf of survivors. His appearances on BBC's Newsnight and Channel 4 News contributed towards the Archbishop of Canterbury resigning after his failings. Never in history had an Archbishop of Canterbury left office like this. Mark continues to appear on TV as he, and other Smyth survivors, work hard for justice.

Mark's hobbies include Lego, and he was, for several years, the official Lego reviewer for *Sorted* Men's Magazine. He runs a popular YouTube Channel devoted to storytelling and faith.

Mark currently lives in Kent with his wife Cherith (from Northern Ireland) and their two Labradors - Bella and Phoebe.

www.markstibbe.com

Winner of the 2020 Page Turner Award for Fiction
MARK STIBBE
A BOOK IN TIME
Available in paperback, hardback and eBook on Amazon.

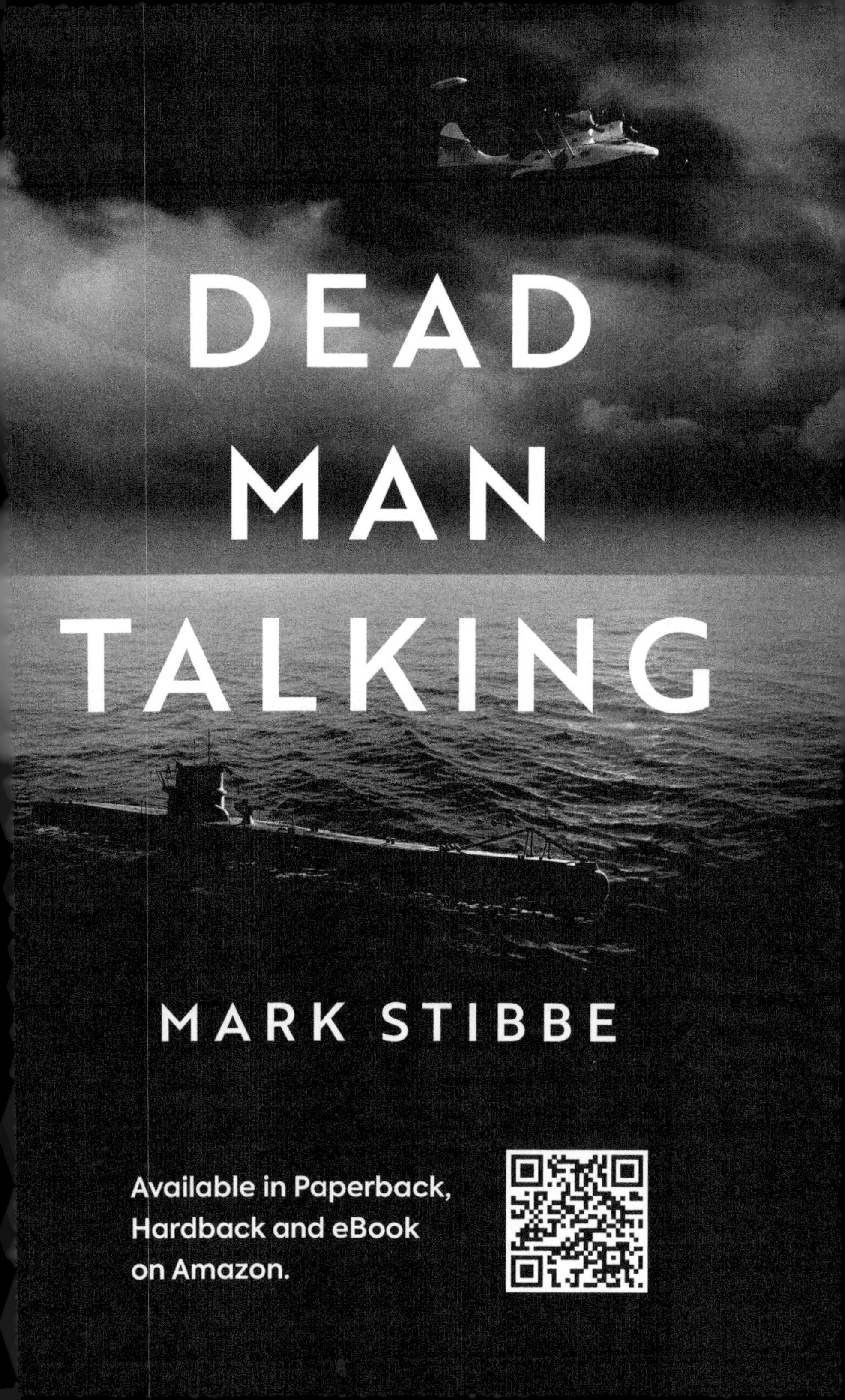
DEAD
MAN
TALKING
MARK STIBBE
Available in Paperback,
Hardback and eBook
on Amazon.

Printed in Great Britain
by Amazon

62557711R00127